Praise for *Waiting for Daisy*

"Moving and bittersweet, *Waiting for Daisy* is as funny, thoughtful, biting, reflective, as filled with fruitful self-doubt and cautious exuberance, as its author."
    —**Michael Chabon, Pulitzer Prize–winning author of** *The Amazing Adventures of Kavalier & Clay*

"An absolutely wonderful book. I couldn't put it down: it reads as easily and yet with as much texture as a novel. As always, Orenstein is both so smart and so human as she tells her story—and ours, too—about her marriage, career, indecision, breast cancer, and whether or not she can, and wants to, and ought to, get pregnant. Sometimes the writing is wrenching, sometimes very funny, but always profoundly honest and engaging."
—Anne Lamott, bestselling author of *Operating Instructions*

"Add to the best literature of motherhood Peggy Orenstein's searing account of her six-year quest to have a child. The story of what she put her body through is beautifully and movingly rendered, but it's her honesty in examining her own mind and heart that make *Waiting for Daisy* such a courageous and unforgettable book. I was enthralled."
    —**Ann Packer, author of** *The Dive from Clausen's Pier*

"A gripping memoir of one woman's quest for a baby…honest, fascinating, and wholly enlightening."
    —**Cathi Hanauer, author of** *Sweet Ruin* **and editor of** *The Bitch in the House*

"Just when you think there is no more to say about the comedy and tragedy of infertility, Peggy Orenstein comes along and changes your mind. This may be the most honest book written about the tsunami of emotion that hits women when what should come most naturally—reproduction—becomes instead one vast, expensive science experiment, and one more likely to fail than not. Orenstein—whose obsession with getting pregnant (after breast cancer and the loss of an ovary, no less) almost derails her career, her marriage and her sanity—is terrific at exploring the struggle of the intellect and the heart: As a feminist, she's always said she won't be defined by motherhood, but there she is in the bathroom, frantically poking her insides to determine if today's cervical mucous is 'gorgeous.' With its startlingly mundane happy ending, *Daisy* is a fine meditation on what it means to live a fulfilled life." —*People*

"*Waiting for Daisy* is riveting...It's no small feat to write a page turner that gives away the ending on the dust jacket, but *Waiting for Daisy* is more than just the Perils of Peggy. Orenstein has written a memoir, a confession, a polemic and a love story all at once, describing the most frantic and confusing period of her life with clarity and candor." —*Los Angeles Times*

"Peggy Orenstein's journey [is] suspenseful [and]...unsparing...the book describes Orenstein's rapid descent into the surreal community of the subfertile...It's to Orenstein's considerable credit that even when she's naked from the waist down, she never really takes her reporter's hat off, applying the same measured scrutiny to a junior-high-school boyfriend with a brood of 15 or the plight of women left barren and disfigured by the atomic bomb dropped on Hiroshima as she does to her own ultimately happily resolved situation...Orenstein's interrogation of her own profiteering pregnancy retinue comes across as a welcome, even necessary exposé." —*New York Times Book Review*

"'*Waiting*' for Daisy? No term as passive as 'waiting' begins to describe how Peggy Orenstein clawed her way to motherhood like a climber scaling Mount Everest in a gale-force blizzard...caustically funny, the author brings alarming frankness to a familiar story of baby lust run amok." —*Boston Globe*

"The story of author Peggy Orenstein's struggle with infertility is riveting, but what really makes her new memoir such a compelling read is her refreshing honesty about the complicated emotions many women face on the path to motherhood."

—Parenting

"A raw, funny and poignant memoir…she writes keenly and with humor about the difficult road her quest takes. By the time I reached the end of the book, I was crying into my latte. Orenstein's memoir is not just hers; it is the story of a generation of women who dared to wait for motherhood, took risks to achieve it and were brave enough to question their decisions every step of the way."

—More

"Funny, self-knowing and sometimes wise…The outcome of this story may seem obvious, but that's less important than how Orenstein gets there."

—Chicago Tribune

"[Orenstein] treats her efforts to become a mother with intelligent skepticism and a brazen sense of humor (a quality not often found in Repro Lit)…Unlike many women who have written about the experience of trying and failing to have a baby, Orenstein doesn't leave her feminism at the door. She writes frankly about her initial reluctance to become a mother and traces the complicated evolution of her feelings from 'no! never!' to single-minded passion. Once launched on the all-consuming path, she makes stops that will be familiar to many of her readers…But her voice makes all the difference in the world. Far from the anguished, often reverential, super-serious tone of Internet discussion groups…One of the best things about this book is that when she succeeds in her quest, Orenstein refuses to take refuge in the smug pieties so prevalent in fertility discussions. When a friend tells her that everything happens for a reason, Orenstein bristles (bless her!)…As Daisy moves on through life, and her mother and father move with her through the parenting maze, it would be interesting to hear Orenstein's intelligent, skeptical voice ruminate on the next stages. For if any writer has the verve and tenacity to supersede the typecasting of Mommy Lit, it's Orenstein."

—Washington Post

"Peggy Orenstein is an accomplished journalist, and she skillfully and vividly tells this tale in which, after eight months of failing to conceive, a very intelligent, well-educated woman succumbs to the blandishments of fertility specialists…she writes far better and more coherently than the other writers of her cohort who have worked this beat, Naomi Wolf and Susan Faludi. She is also more humorous…She is never less than good at portraying the 'descent into the world of infertility'…unlike Faludi and Wolf, Orenstein can think enough outside the feminist box…Stay tuned for the next installment." —*First Things*

"The author has a curious, tenacious mind and a courageous spirit, both of which are much in evidence here. But what makes the book really riveting is the spectacle of Orenstein—a devoted, polemical feminist—coming to terms with her powerful need to be a mother…[a] painfully honest journey…She tells the truth about it, and in doing so gives us a complex, endearing and deeply feminist book."
—*Raleigh News and Observer*

"You don't have to be coping with infertility yourself to fall in love with Orenstein's memoir of the long and difficult road to parenthood…Her persona is irresistible. She is funny, irreverent, blunt and ever aware of what is happening to her mentally and physically." —*Arizona Republic*

"Ebullient, heart-wrenching, and honest, *Daisy* delves into how the pain of trying to conceive can fray even the happiest marriage. Part of Orenstein's genius is how she stretches her subject like a rubber band to write engagingly about single-by-choice Japanese women (they're called 'parasites'), rituals marking miscarriage and abortion, and the courage of a Hiroshima survivor whose face was destroyed. Funny and wise, *Waiting for Daisy* is a page-turning delight." —*Cookie*

"Orenstein's account of her six-year quest to have a child (with multiple miscarriages and rounds of IVF treatments) will have you in awe of her resolve—and cheering when her baby finally arrives." —*Life*

"Inspiration and solace come in copious quantities in Peggy Orenstein's dazzling new memoir, a heart-rending account of her six-year quest to conceive a child. [Orenstein] recounts an Olympian odyssey to motherhood that includes daunting obstacles (three miscarriages, breast cancer, infertility treatments, alternate therapies, possible adoption, an imperiled marriage) while also racing along with the pulse-pounding tenseness of a thriller. So remarkable is Orenstein's account that it seems likely to become the platinum standard for memoirs regarding couples struggling to become parents. *Waiting for Daisy* becomes instant required reading for them and those who follow them down that hope-laden pathway with so many confounding forks…Orenstein does an excellent job in describing the progression of medical treatments during her quest, what they promised, what they entailed, how they felt. But the greatest strength of her memoir is her resounding ability to surmount the far greater writing challenge—capturing the rocky emotional landscape she and her husband traversed…*Waiting for Daisy* accomplishes many valuable things in just 226 pages. But one of the most valuable is fostering profound respect and empathy for couples who endure great struggles trying to become parents." —*Seattle Post-Intelligencer*

"[A] startling and touching memoir."
—*Milwaukee Journal Sentinel*

"[A] funny, honest new book…Fertility issues have become Topic A; even the Dixie Chicks have a song about it. Orenstein's chronicle of her baby obsession is both quirkily her own and in tune with the moment." —*San Francisco Chronicle*

"Her book is a startling portrait of how the quest to deliver a baby in this brave new world of 'endless' fertility can derail even the most confident, accomplished woman."
—*San Jose Mercury News*

"Her painfully candid and moving memoir deftly wipes the Vaseline coating off the lens of modern motherhood and exposes it for the messy business it is."

—*Minneapolis Star-Tribune*

"Orenstein...bares her soul in *Waiting for Daisy*, opening old wounds and giving readers a frank look into her personal, at times heart-wrenching journey to motherhood."

—*Contra Costa Times*

"The *Rocky* of infertility memoirs." —*New York* magazine

"If you have thrown your dreams of parenthood into the chill of the laboratory, this book will bring every memory to the surface. If you are thinking about supplementing old-fashioned procreation with science, this book is a good field-guide to what lies ahead. And if you are a woman in your 30s, this book should ring like a warning bell in the night—at 37, you move into the 'elderly gravid' cohort, and the chances that you'll become a mother start to drop dramatically."

—**HeadButler.com**

"Orenstein...brings her erudition and intelligence to bear on her own experience." —*San Francisco* magazine

"Orenstein renders her experience in beautiful prose."

—*Entertainment Weekly*

"Intimate, funny/sad and remarkably self-revealing."

—*Kirkus Reviews* (starred review)

"While readers don't have to be fertility-obsessed to enjoy this very witty memoir, for the growing number of women struggling with infertility this book may become their new best friend." —*Publishers Weekly*

WAITING FOR DAISY

By the same author

*Flux: Women on Sex, Work, Love, Kids, and Life in a
Half-Changed World*

Schoolgirls: Young Women, Self-Esteem, and the Confidence Gap

WAITING FOR DAISY

A Tale of Two Continents, Three Religions, Five Infertility Doctors, an Oscar®, an Atomic Bomb, a Romantic Night, and One Woman's Quest to Become a Mother

PEGGY ORENSTEIN

BLOOMSBURY

Copyright © 2007 by Peggy Orenstein

Published by Bloomsbury USA, New York
Distributed to the trade by Holtzbrinck Publishers

All papers used by Bloomsbury USA are natural,
recyclable products made from wood grown in well-managed forests.
The manufacturing processes conform to the environmental
regulations of the country of origin.

Portions of this book appeared in altered form in the *New York Times Magazine*.

THE LIBRARY OF CONGRESS HAS CATALOGED THE HARDCOVER EDITION AS FOLLOWS:

Orenstein, Peggy.
Waiting for Daisy : a tale of two continents, three religions, five infertility doctors, an Oscar®, an atomic bomb, a romantic night, and one woman's quest to become a mother / Peggy Orenstein. — 1st U.S. ed.
p. cm.
ISBN-13: 978-1-59691-017-1 (alk. paper) (hardcover)
ISBN-10: 1-59691-017-8 (alk. paper) (hardcover)
1. Orenstein, Peggy. 2. Infertility, Female—Patients—United States—Biography.
3. Fertilization in vitro, Human—Popular works. 4. Human reproductive
technology—Popular works. I. Title.

RG201.O74 2006
618.1'780092—dc22
[B]
2006016627

First published by Bloomsbury USA in 2007
This paperback edition published in 2008

Paperback ISBN-10: 1-59691-210-3
ISBN-13: 978-1-59691-210-6

1 3 5 7 9 10 8 6 4 2

Typeset by Westchester Book Group
Printed in the United States of America by Quebecor World Fairfield

For SP & D, of course

CONTENTS

WAITING FOR DAISY

PROLOGUE: THE RECKONING

———•———

I had twenty-four hours to fight for my life; twenty-four hours to right all the wrongs I'd done over the last year, to prove the sincerity of my remorse. If I couldn't, I'd be dead by the following fall. That's the theory, anyway, behind Yom Kippur, the Day of Atonement, the holiest day of the year for Jews. It's the day that God supposedly determines our fate, using indelible ink to inscribe us in the book of Life or the book of Death. When I was a child, growing up in a tightly knit Conservative Jewish community in Minneapolis, it terrified me to think that my destiny would be sealed with the setting sun. As the day faded, the prayers of the adults around me would grow more frenzied, more pleading. The cantor would prostrate himself on the pulpit, his voice ululating. The rabbi would teeter on his feet, having stood before us all day without food or drink. During the last hour, we'd all stand, lights out, arc door open, the Torahs glittering in their New Year's finery. The more devout men lifted their prayer shawls over their heads like shrouds, rocking and moaning, lost in private negotiation for their souls.

I'd long since rejected the rituals as superstition, allowing no room for free will. At best, I'd become an indifferent Jew. But this year, the year I turned forty, I felt desperate for a new beginning. For the first time in over two decades—since leaving my home for Cleveland, New York, and, eventually, Northern California—I fasted, went to the temple dressed in white, a symbol of both death and rebirth. I wore canvas sneakers rather than leather. I didn't bathe or brush my teeth. And I prayed—not to a bearded dude in the sky who was totting up who'd been naughty and who'd been nice, but in hopes of something else: the strength to forgive myself for the sins against my marriage and my own heart that I'd committed during my six-year, single-minded quest to bear a child, and the courage to close my own book, one way or another, on this anguished chapter of my life.

The congregation turned to the pivotal prayer of the day, an alphabetized compendium of sins that they may have committed over the previous year. For something that's centuries old, it's eerily astute. *We have been guilty*, it begins. *We have been hypocritical. We have broken our standards of behavior. We have given bad advice. We have been hardheaded. We have misled others. We have misled ourselves.* After each admission we were to pound our chests with closed fists. *Forgive us, pardon us, allow us to atone.*

As my neighbors in the pews confessed, I silently made my own reckoning—a list of offenses that had begun inconsequentially then snowballed into a betrayal of my deepest self: I'd taken my temperature every morning. *I have been obsessive.* I'd peed on ovulation predictors five days a month. I'd craned my neck like a yogini to see my nether regions while sluicing my finger around to check for the monthly fluid that would guide sperm to egg. *I have been impatient.* I'd chugged bottles of cough syrup, whose active ingredient supposedly improves the flow. I'd interrupted lovemaking to squirt egg whites into myself with a turkey baster, also a flow enhancer. I'd stood on my head post-coitally until I thought my neck would snap. *I have humiliated myself.* I'd rushed to my doctor's after an afternoon quickie so she could examine my husband's and my commingled juices under a microscope. I'd transported cups of sperm in my bra. I'd turned lovemaking soulless, insisting my husband watch porn to speed things up, coming in to "do his business" when he was ready. *Pardon me, forgive me, allow me to atone.*

I'd taken ovulation-stimulating pills that triggered fits of rage. *I have been wicked.* I'd given myself multiple daily injections of fertility drugs despite my breast cancer diagnosis a few years earlier. *I have made mistakes.* I'd asked my parents for twenty-five thousand dollars for long-shot in vitro fertilization treatments. I'd let someone stick pins into my body every two weeks for a year and downed unidentifiable herbal potions that tasted like dirt. *I have been disappointed.* I'd believed in the next new thing. *I have allowed myself to be led astray.* I'd waited too long to start trying to conceive. Had I waited too long to start trying to conceive? *Pardon me, forgive me, allow me to atone.*

I'd had no idea how easy it would be to lose all sense of reason, to do things I swore I never would to become a mother, then go further beyond that. And here's the irony: if you'd asked me ten years earlier, I would've said I didn't even want to have children.

1

TO HAVE OR HAVE NOT

My first birthday, Thanksgiving 1962. My aunts, uncles, and cousins are all in attendance. I am wearing a blue velvet dress, my chubby legs stuffed into white tights; my feet, which have yet to master walking, strapped into patent leather Mary Janes. A few pale, wispy curls are beginning to sprout on my head, though I don't have any hair worth mentioning. My mother has compensated by taping a blue bow to my pate, which I periodically rip off and stuff into my mouth.

As a Bell & Howell whirs, I tear into my birthday gifts, more focused on shredding the brightly colored paper than on the toys that lay within. My father steps into the frame, his hair still black, his face hopeful. He is seven years younger than I am now. Clearly excited, he presents me with my first baby doll, placing it in my arms. I am his only daughter. I glance at the doll, frown, and fling it out of sight. He fetches it and once again, patiently, sets it in my arms. This time I begin to cry and hold the doll by its foot, dropping it on the floor. My father tries one more time with similar results; the camera jerks and the image sputters.

What happened then, during those undocumented moments? Someone must've continued to cajole. Someone must've expressed disappointment. Someone must've demonstrated what was expected of me. Someone must've said, "Don't you want to be a mommy, like Mommy?" Because when the film rolls again, I gingerly cradle the baby doll, still sniffling a little, seeming anxious. I look up eagerly for approval from my parents, who are squatting next to me. This is my first foray into motherhood.

At eleven, I befriended Tibetha Shaw, who had untamed orange hair and was the only girl in the sixth grade of John Burroughs Elementary School to wear black all the time. Her mother, unlike those of the rest of my friends, worked outside the home and had an apron that read HOUSEWORK IS BULLSHIT in three-inch capital letters. At the Shaws' there was dust on the furniture. There was no adult supervision after school. Tibetha and I gorged on store-bought cookies and pored over *Ms.* magazine, which had recently resurrected the comic book icon Wonder Woman. Inspired by her, we fastened towels around our necks with clothespins and—in every working mom's nightmare of what the kids are up to in her absence—climbed a ladder onto the roof of the garage. The distance to the next building was slightly longer than a leggy eleven-year-old's stride, yet we took deep breaths and leapt—screaming, "WONDER

WOMAN! WONDER WOMAN!"—flying from roof to roof and back again, towel capes streaming behind us. It was my first foray into feminism.

My understanding of the women's movement may have grown more nuanced over the years, but that sense of exhilaration remained. Feminism provided me with an escape route, an out from my parents' limited expectations, a chance to define for myself the person I wanted to be. Yet, even while soaring through space—whether the rooftops were real or metaphoric—I was conscious of the drop, never quite sure how far my towel cape would carry me. As an editorial assistant at *Esquire* magazine, I was peanut gallery to 1980s literary New York, an extra at cocktail parties for the likes of Jay McInerney, Tom Wolfe, and Tama Janowitz. Occasionally, while stuffing myself with free hors d'oeuvres (popping a few in my purse to supplement my $250 a week paycheck), I'd notice that there weren't many mothers in the room. There were few among the editors I worked with either, and virtually none among the writers. The same was true several years later, when I moved on to San Francisco. Their absence left me vaguely uneasy; was this evidence of progress—women no longer needed children for fulfillment—or its opposite? Could it be that things hadn't changed as much as I'd thought? And if they hadn't, in which world did I belong? "I'm not sure I want to have kids," I told my friends. "I'm not sure I want to have kids," I told my gynecologist. "I'm not sure I want to have kids," I told my editor. (She fixed my manuscripts, why not my life?) They all gave the same reply: "Don't worry about it, Peggy, you have plenty of time."

I believed them; I was in my mid-twenties. I thought I had all the time in the world.

I fell in love with Steven Okazaki on a postcard. We'd gone on one date, an after-work drink that deepened into dinner, but it hadn't gone well. I was newly out of a bruising relationship and knocked back a couple of Stolis to calm my nerves. Here's something to know about me: I can't hold my liquor. As my rational self watched from a helpless, anesthetized distance, my soused evil twin ran her mouth, spewing bile about former beaux and announcing, "If you're looking for anything serious, I'm not interested."

Luckily, he didn't believe me. "Women always say that kind of stuff when they like you," he'd joke later. We hugged good-bye awkwardly in the parking lot. A documentary filmmaker, Steven was leaving the next day for a shoot on the Big Island of Hawaii. "Call me!" I chirped, though after my performance that evening I figured I'd never hear from him again.

Then the card arrived, a photo of the lava flow on Mt. Kilauea. On the back, a note, jotted as if we were mid-conversation.

Last night on the Big Island there was a bad storm. Several boats were beached and sections of highway were temporarily washed out. I was having dinner with a pig breeder and his family near a town called Honaunau. The sound of the wind and rain on their tin roof was nearly deafening. The farmer noted that the roads would get dangerous and maybe I should spend the night. He said, "You can wear my pajamas and sleep in the kitchen." I thought, "No way, man. I want my hotel room." As I took the perilous journey home, I felt ashamed but frankly relieved. One doesn't have to experience everything, does one?

Forget roses; I'm a sucker for a man who has a way with words. We shared our first breakfast shortly after he returned, gazing starry-eyed at each other across our eggs in a Berkeley diner. Steven was tall and stocky with a shock of black hair that was just beginning to gray, diamond-cut cheekbones, and eyes as warm as anything I'd ever seen. I loved the scratch in his voice, the touch of his skin, his dedication to a life of purpose and creativity. I admired the confidence he had in his own vision; I was still a magazine editor then, unable to work up the nerve to quit and write full-time. Steven was not the man I imagined I'd be with—nearly ten years older, Japanese American, a gentile—but soul mates don't always come in predictable packages.

He mentioned he'd grown up with four sisters. "I always thought I'd have a big family," he said.

I cut him off. "Well, I don't know if I want to have children at all."

"Really? Why not?"

"Why do you *want* them?"

This was when I first discovered my future husband's habit of speaking in set pieces. "I guess I think of life as kind of like an amusement park," he said. "If you're going to go, you should ride every ride at least once. And having kids is like the big, scary roller coaster. You can have a good time without riding it, but you would've missed a significant part of the experience."

"I get sick on roller coasters," I deadpanned, then added, "Besides, 'One doesn't have to experience everything, does one?'"

He raised an eyebrow.

"Look," I said. "I don't want anyone to make any assumptions about me or how I'll live my life. I don't want to do something just because it's expected, because everyone else does it. Maybe I'll change my mind, but there are a lot of other things I want to do besides have children."

"There's no way I can have a baby now." It had been two years since Steven and I had married, since I'd moved across the Great Waters from my overpriced apartment in San Francisco to his rent-controlled one in Berkeley. I'd simultaneously taken the leap into writing; my first book, *Schoolgirls*, about the challenges young women face in their teens, had just come out to flattering reviews. Suddenly I was fielding calls from *Good Morning America*, *Nightline*, and *Fresh Air*; lecturing at universities; giving keynote addresses at national conferences. My agent—a forceful, older woman who'd opted against motherhood—warned me, "You have to sell another book idea *right now*. If you wait a year, forget it. No one will remember you." I'd dreamed of this kind of success since publishing my first story in my high school newspaper at age fifteen. But I wasn't fifteen anymore. I was thirty-two.

How could I possibly cut back to take care of an infant? Sometime later, Joyce Purnick, Metro editor of the *New York Times* (who did not have kids), would tell graduating seniors at Barnard, "If I had left the *Times* to have children and then come back to work a four-day week . . . or left the office at six o'clock instead of eight or nine, I wouldn't be Metro editor." She was probably right, but how grim was that? Maybe I wanted children, maybe I didn't, but I wanted the decision to be a choice, not a mandate. Last time I checked, childlessness was only supposed to be a condition of career advancement for nuns.

My own mother was no help. She had married at twenty, moving directly from her parents' home to her new life with her twenty-four-year-old husband. Within five years she'd stopped teaching elementary school to raise her children. We shared so little experience that without a child myself, I sometimes felt as if we were, if not a different species, at least different sexes. "Your life is so unlike mine," she'd say. "I can't even imagine it." I longed for a mother who could be a mentor, someone I could turn to for wisdom and guidance. Her limits made me short-tempered. *Stop being such a bitch*, I'd tell myself, which only turned my anger to guilt. *I'd rather not have children*, I'd think, *than have a daughter who someday felt this way about me*.

That's too easy, though. It wasn't just hostility I felt around my mother, it was inadequacy. I had loved my early childhood with her. We'd spent long hours playing beauty parlor and tea party, baking holiday cookies. On Saturday nights I would swoon when she left with my dad in a cloud of Rive Gauche perfume, so glamorous in her fox-trimmed coat. I wanted to be just like her—a mommy just like Mommy. Thirty years later, part of me still did. Although I publicly stood up for working mothers and day care, I knew that, for me, motherhood meant one thing: being there for your children like my mom had been there for me. I believed the responsibility for taking care of children would, bottom line, be mine, even if I was the one who had to swap my dreams for drudgery. It didn't matter that Steven expected to be an equal parent. ("I'll make a great mom," he'd brag.) The issue wasn't whether I wanted to turn into my mother if I had a child or even whether I feared I would; it was that I believed I *should*.

With Steven, I dodged the subject. "We'll talk about it later," I'd promise when he brought it up. "When we have more time." Or: "When I'm not traveling so much." Or: "When we're on vacation." Or: "At the end of the year." Or, simply: "Not now." There was no way he could pin me down. I bobbed, I weaved, I changed the subject, and if none of that worked, I gave him The Stare. "You have no idea how hard it is to get past that look," he'd complain, though of course I did. The Stare had taken me years to perfect: it was my force field, repelling all comers—my parents, lovers, friends, colleagues—who broached a subject that felt too raw to discuss.

The only time in twenty years that I ever had a fight with my friend Robin was at a girls' night dinner party on New York's Upper West Side, when I mouthed off about mothers who dropped their careers rather than demand that their husbands do the laundry. I was in town doing interviews for my next book, *Flux*, about how women make their personal and professional choices. A group of full-time moms I'd talked to that afternoon had claimed that staying home was a feminist right. I disagreed. "I don't know why women who make the pre–Betty Freidan choices think they won't end up with the pre–Betty Freidan results," I quipped.

"What about me?" asked Robin, sharply. She'd been a television news producer before staying home with her three kids.

11

Her husband managed a hedge fund. "Is that what you think of me?"

I wasn't sure how to respond; the truth was, yes, I did feel that way about her, though I'd never say so to her face. My hesitation only made her madder. "You have no idea what it means to be married to someone who works twelve hours a day. If I kept working, I'd still have to do everything at home. It's just not realistic."

"I'm not stupid," she added. "I know the potential traps here. I knew what I was getting into. And I *chose* this."

"But how much of a choice is it," I asked, "if nothing else seemed possible?"

Nearly all of my girlfriends were having children, and one by one, like Robin, they'd dropped out of the workforce. The minds that once produced sparkling prose or defended abused children were now obsessed with picking the right preschool or competing to throw the most elaborate Pocahontas birthday party. Sometimes they seemed to me like something out of *Invasion of the Body Snatchers*. Who were these women and what had they done with my friends? Sure, a few were content, but most, if not exactly unhappy, seemed trapped—fretting over what they'd do when the kids were older, worried that they'd never escape the stroller set. I was disappointed by how readily they'd fallen on the sword of traditional motherhood, how reluctant they were to assert their needs, how loath to rock the boat of their husbands' careers. They weren't the role models I wanted—needed—them to be. These were, after all, women I loved and respected. If they couldn't make it all work, how could I?

My working mom friends weren't much better, perpetually

exhausted and resentful. One commented that Steven and I had the best marriage she knew. "That's because we don't have kids," I said, laughing, but I meant it. Steven and I had a great time together, traveling to Hawaii, Asia, and Europe; going to the movies; spending the weekend in bed. He read the first drafts of my articles; I watched the rough cuts of his films. He was my best friend. Maybe a baby would bring us even closer, but that wasn't what I saw around me. So many women were smitten with their children while begrudging everything their husbands did or didn't do: Kids may have been the glue holding couples together, but they were also the wedge driving them apart.

And yet. There were moments when I could almost feel the weight of a child in my arms, when I sensed that if I looked over my shoulder while driving, I would see an infant seat with a curly-haired bundle looking back at me. I would imagine the songs we'd sing together, the games we'd play, the books we'd read. Pasting photos into an album, I would recall leafing through old pictures of my mother, my father, my grandparents. Who would see these? Who would care?

One night, when I was thirty-three, I walked into the living room of our rented house in the rustic (read: lots of weeds, aggressive deer, druggie neighbors) Berkeley Hills. Steven was lying on the couch reading *Mojo*, a British music rag for guys who own everything—on vinyl—that the Kinks ever recorded. The floor beneath him slanted steeply for reasons that in Northern California were best not to consider; he had put shims of varying heights under all the furniture to make it appear level. On the upside, the house was large, with three ample bedrooms, two of which were glaringly empty.

"What do you think of the name 'Cleo' for a baby?" I asked him.

He put down the magazine and sat up. "Peg, we don't *have* a baby."

"Well, maybe we should."

"Really?" he said, skeptically. "Is that what you want?"

"I don't know," I sighed. "Maybe we shouldn't."

He shook his head, dramatically picking up his magazine. "Let me know when you want to talk about having a baby and *then* I'll talk about names."

"Okay," I said, "so what do *you* think we should do?"

"I don't want to do it unless we both want to. I don't want you ever to say, 'You talked me into this.' And if you don't want to do it, I'll be fine. I won't have that many regrets." It was all very self-actualized, very reasonable, except for this: punting the decision back to me effectively let Steven off the hook. He, too, put a premium on freedom, the time to pursue creative work, to travel, and, in his case, to lie on the couch reading *Mojo*. This was a guy who had stayed single until he was forty; he wasn't so eager himself to take on the responsibilities and lifestyle of parenting. My indecision played neatly—maybe too neatly—into his own.

Another year ticked by and I remained chronically, maddeningly conflicted, no closer than ever to untangling what others expected of me from what I'd learned to want from my genuine desire. I was clear about who I *didn't* want to be like, but not who I *did*. So many people I knew—women and men—had tumbled into their lives without much thought, defaulted into marriages, careers, and parenthood because that was what one was supposed to do. I wanted to live my life more consciously. But what did that mean? How could I guess what I might regret in twenty years? How could I say a definite "no" to motherhood while it was still a biological possibility? How could I know who that long-ago girl might've been if no one had pressed that doll into her arms?

"Peg, I want to talk to you about something."

Steven and I were cruising thirty-eight thousand feet above the Pacific, flying back from his father's funeral in Los Angeles. It was late November, the end of a lousy year. A few months earlier one of Steven's best friends, a woman in her early forties, had also died, of ovarian cancer, leaving behind her husband and three-year-old daughter. There had been other losses, too, friends taken by AIDS or cancer. I had just turned thirty-five. I was beginning to realize what it meant to be a grown-up.

If my father-in-law hadn't died, we might have never resolved whether to have a child; we might have drifted on—me avoiding the topic, Steven allowing that—until time made the decision for us. But grief had burned away his doubt.

"We're on an airplane," I said, warily, recognizing the tone in his voice.

"I know. So there's nothing to distract us." He took a deep breath, raked a hand through his hair. "It's just that I lost one of my best friends and now I've lost my dad. And I'm starting to feel like we're not part of the life cycle, like we're not participating. When there's been so much death, it seems like there should be birth. We should to do something life-affirming. I think we should have a child."

15

Maybe my defenses were down, or I, too, had been humbled by loss. Or maybe I had wanted him to make the decision all along. But that simple argument was all it took to tip the scales inside my heart. "Okay," I said. "Let's do it. Let's have a baby."

"Really?" he said softly, taking my hand. "Do you mean it?"

I nodded. "Yes," I said, "I mean it." We giggled like kids sharing a secret until I added: "How about if I go off the Pill in June? That would give me six months to finish the reporting for my book, then I can write it while I'm pregnant."

Steven's eyes flashed. "I want to do it," I insisted, "It's just . . . I need more time."

"You can't keep putting this off," he said. "You can't schedule life to happen only when it's convenient." He sank back into his seat, staring out the window until the plane touched down.

My friend Connie once told me she got pregnant with her son because, "It started to feel like someone who was supposed to be in the house was missing." For the rest of the day, I tested that notion, played with it, tried to imagine that absent person, that anticipatory space. I found that while my ambivalence didn't disappear, I could indeed do it. Maybe I was one of those people who would never know for sure, who just had to take a leap of faith.

"I mean it," I whispered to Steven as we snuggled close that night. "Let's have a baby."

Six weeks later, I was diagnosed with breast cancer.

On January 16, 1997, at 4:45 P.M. my surgeon told me over the phone that the tissue she'd removed from my breast to biopsy was malignant. I was puttering around my office in the house we'd bought a few months earlier, a scandalously priced two-bedroom whose garage, if need be, could be converted into a third. I'd forgotten the doctor was scheduled to call; I was about to head out with Steven to a movie. At the sound of her voice all the colors in the room went flat. The abnormality had been caught two weeks earlier on my first mammogram, the one I'd had as a baseline, as part of clearing the decks before trying to get pregnant. No one, not the surgeon, not the radiologist, expected this. *It can't be true*, I thought as I listened to her. *I'm only thirty-five years old. I don't have a family history of cancer.* I did, however, have a history of reproductive tumors; I'd had an ovary removed in my teens when a benign cyst was discovered on it during my first pelvic exam. (In a miracle of compensation, the other one took over, popping out an egg each month.) She assured me that was unrelated. What's more, she added, this new invader was small, still too small to feel, and slow growing. The chances that I would survive it, with a lumpectomy and six weeks of daily radiation treatments, were upward of 90 percent.

"But what about kids? Can I still have kids?" We could talk about that later, she said. I'd certainly have to put pregnancy off for a year, maybe two. Right now, though, we had to focus on getting rid of the disease.

"You're a very lucky woman," she added.

"*Lucky?*" I wanted to shout. "*Fuck you!*" Instead, I thanked her politely and hung up.

Steven was by now standing in the doorway of my office, listening on the extension. We stared at each other in the waning winter light. "But I eat organic broccoli," I wailed, and burst into tears.

17

That night I woke at 3 A.M. in a sweat, imagining my death and realizing I'd made a terrible mistake. I'd become the woman in that Lichtenstein spoof, an assemblage of dots and halftones who—Oops!—forgot to have children. How could I have been so stupid? Why didn't I realize how much I wanted a baby until the possibility was threatened? Later I would remember that moment as the first time that I was ready but my body said no. You can't believe it, not in this age when we control so much of our own destinies. I fumbled for a pen and notebook in the dark: "Am I being punished?" I scrawled. "For what? Being on the Pill? Waiting to have children? My independence?"

Over the next few months, my life went into a fugue state. Mostly I stared out my office window, watching the light play across the redwood trees, letting the days go by me. My friends and family were impressed by how well I was coping, but my composure was an act. Although my prognosis was good—I didn't even need chemotherapy—getting cancer at such a young age didn't bode well for the future. *I might die*, I thought over and over, *I really might die*. All I wanted in that heightened, crystalline state was to have a child. I tried to take comfort in the knowledge that the cancer may have been in my body for years and the hormonal changes of pregnancy could've accelerated it, made it more deadly, but that didn't help. Sometimes my grief was so intense it made my lungs ache.

My oncologist was reassuring. Although, at the time, there was data on only six hundred women in the entire world who'd been pregnant after cancer, he didn't think it would affect my long-term survival. In other words, if I wasn't going to die anyway, having a baby probably wouldn't kill me. He suggested I wait six months to recover from the radiation treatment, but not let cancer hold me back, not let it define me. "You don't want to feel like you're sick," he said. "That's what cancer is about: realizing how fragile life is, but because you're aware of that, enjoying life, seizing it with both hands. And for you, that includes having a baby.

"So go," he added, "be fruitful and multiply."

A friend once said she'd been "visiting her terror" lately, as if it were a geographical place. All that summer and into the fall, I found myself visiting my terror, too, at unexpected moments—during a busy workday, for instance, or over dinner with friends. I'd think, *I'm a thirty-five-year-old who just had cancer.* It seemed simultaneously unreal and the most real thing there was. But something else happened as the months passed, too. I began to trust that I would indeed survive, and as I did my regret about missing my chance at motherhood receded. Simply being alive and being with Steven seemed enough. The old ambivalence even began to seep back. Which were my true feelings? The anguish I'd felt facing death, or the uncertainty I'd felt all my life?

My thirty-sixth birthday fell the Saturday before Thanksgiving. It had been a year since Steven's father had died, a year since we'd first decided to try to have a baby. I had gone off the Pill as a safety precaution after my cancer diagnosis. Now I took a deep breath, closed my eyes, and threw away my diaphragm as well.

I still wasn't sure it was the right thing to do.

2

IF AT FIRST . . .

I married a man who is far better looking than I. It's not that I'm a candidate for a dogfight, exactly, but no one's ever going to confuse me with Adriana Lima. Steven, meanwhile, was once plastered on billboards all over America as part of a Gap campaign, the one featuring artsy types who embodied "cool." At a screening of one of his films at the Smithsonian, a young woman bustled up to say that the ladies of Harvard's Asian Pacific American Law Students Association had hung his picture in their office for "inspiration." ("Hi!" I said brightly, cutting in front of him. "I'm his wife.") He is largely indifferent to such flattery. Having lived with it all his life, he understands the power of beauty, the privilege it confers, and he understands its limits. Still, I've often marveled at the idea that he was handsome in junior high, a time when my acne was blessedly obscured by the twin glares off my braces and glasses. On our third date I showed Steven a snapshot of me in college, zaftig in a peasant skirt and my boyfriend's ill-fitting crewneck sweater, my hair cut to resemble a Semitic cotton ball. It was part of what made him fall in love with me. "I thought it was brave of you to show me something that embarrassing," he said later. "Brave, and kind of pathetic."

There is only one thing about me that anyone has ever considered gorgeous. Three different gynecologists have, upon intimate examination, invoked that word to describe my cervical mucous. I would have no trouble getting pregnant, they always informed me. I didn't know at the time, nor much care, what cervical mucous was, but I would blush modestly anyway, not that they could see from their vantage point. I had reason, then, to think conception would be a snap—my gorgeous mucous would assure it. Besides, I deserved something to go smoothly with my body—it would be a way to rebalance the scales of fate after cancer treatment. And so we began to try.

There is the first time you have sex, and then there is the first time you have sex without birth control. On purpose. To make a baby. Both events feel transformative, but this time I didn't feel the urge to jump up and phone my best friend when it was over. There was something both sacred and carnal about the way Steven and I joined together during those early nights, an erotic thrill in breaking the taboo against unprotected sex, along with a startling intimacy. It was as if a wall between us, sheer as gossamer, had come down. I touched Steven's cheek as his hands traced circles down my body. "Here we go," I whispered and he smiled. We were making something more than love: we were making our child. I already felt pregnant with possibility.

Three months went by—not a long time, but I've always trended toward the anxious. I'd also known a number of couples, including my oldest brother and his wife, who'd had difficulty conceiving. A friend suggested the book *Taking Charge of Your Fertility.* "Taking Charge": she was speaking my language. The book explained that a woman doesn't necessarily ovulate on the fourteenth day of her cycle—you might ovulate on the twelfth. Or the twentieth. When you do, the egg lives twenty-four hours, max, but sperm can lounge around in your body for up to five days. It's strategic, then, to have lots of sex *before* you ovulate so the guys are up there, ready and waiting, when the ball drops. Doing it after ovulation, or even during, may be too late. What's more, there are signs that a woman's critical time is nigh. That cervical mucous my doctors swooned over? It miraculously transforms in the days before ovulation to a clear, come-hither liquid—similar to semen—that helps speed sperm to egg. I'd had my period for almost a quarter of a century. During college I'd lay on a dormitory floor with a bunch of other women "empowering" ourselves by looking up our yin-yangs with plastic specula and hand mirrors. I thought I knew the facts of life. (Natalie's gay and Tootie starred in *The Vagina Monologues*, right?) Yet I didn't know any of this.

So I began to take charge. I popped a thermometer into my mouth every morning before so much as kissing Steven hello. I plotted my temperature on a graph I'd Xeroxed from the book, carefully connected it to the dots of previous days, and pored over the results like they were rune stones. Had the temperature gone up more than two-tenths of a point since the day before? Had it stayed up for three days, indicating that I'd ovulated and the procreative window had slammed shut? I spent an enormous amount of time in the bathroom poking my fingers up my vagina. Was my cervix open and low? High and closed? Was that even my cervix? Was my "fluid" (as *Taking Charge* referred to it—so much cozier than *mucous*) sticky? Creamy? The coveted clear and stretchy? Most of the time it looked to me like gunk. I peed on ovulation predictor sticks but couldn't tell when the second line was the precise shade of magenta as the first. Sometimes, to be sure, I'd go through several sticks in an afternoon.

I quit drinking coffee, though I'd never drunk more than two cups a day, and substituted two teaspoons of Robitussin each morning. Its main ingredient, guaifenesin, thins and loosens mucous in the lungs, and although there is no actual evidence, it's thought to work similar juju farther south. Meanwhile, *Taking Charge* warned that lubricants—including saliva—could kill sperm, so I tossed out the Astroglide and foreswore oral sex; if the going got rough, I squirted warmed egg whites (another of semen's cousins) inside me with a turkey baster. To add to the fun, I limited us to the missionary position, which, according to the book, was the most gravitationally correct.

"You're turning this into a military maneuver," Steven groused one morning as I studied my charts. He glanced at his wrist like he was synchronizing a watch. "Operation Baby."

"There's no point in trying if we're doing it at the wrong time," I said without looking up.

"But you don't have to be so clinical about it. It's bad karma to try to create a child this way. It won't work."

"That's ridiculous," I lectured him. Pregnancy was a scientific equation: sperm and egg. It was a matter of timing. Enjoying the process would be nice, but it wasn't essential. "I'm thirty-six years old," I said. "We can be romantic the rest of the month."

My friend Diane places a symbol of what she calls her "heart's desire" on her bedside table. She'd been through five in the past six years—including a business card when she was hoping for a promotion, and a peace button when her husband was quarreling with his siblings—and they'd all paid off. She claims that a friend of a friend with a fireman fixation tried it with a photo of a 9/11 hero she'd ripped from a magazine; soon she had a one-legged boyfriend. The connection? In the picture, one of the fireman's gams was obscured by a hydrant. A girl has to watch out for such things.

"That might be apocryphal," Diane admitted. "But to me, the symbol is a nightly reminder of what you want. I'd like to think it's magic, but it's really more like a form of prayer. Then you work on it unconsciously in your dreams. And when you wake up each morning, you focus on the symbol again when your mind is still free from the clutter of the day."

I took stock of my nightstand. There was a broken sand dollar from a long-ago trip to Big Sur (I'd pushed the pieces together so it looked whole, because I liked the pattern); an inlaid pillbox from a stoner ex-boyfriend; an antique pocket watch from a childhood pal who'd replaced the face with my fourth-grade school picture. *Jeez*, I thought. *Broken shells? Gifts from exes? Stopped time? What was I thinking?* I swept them into the trash and assembled a more conducive shrine: a Lakota soapstone turtle that I'd picked up on a visit to South Dakota and later learned was a fertility symbol; a turquoise bear from Santa

Fe (I was trying to *bear* a child); a balsa-wood box of brightly dressed Guatemalan worry dolls, the kind that are said to solve your troubles while you sleep.

At first Steven was amused; he liked my little display so much that he moved it to the living room. "Where are my animals?" I said, aghast, that night.

"I thought they'd look better in the other room," he said.

"I do *not* want them moved."

"I just thought . . ."

I glared at him. "I do *not* want them moved," I repeated, carefully setting them back in their places. "I can't believe you touched them."

"Jesus, Peg. Next you'll be putting voodoo dolls under the bed."

"I already have," I said, primly. I lifted the comforter to show him the beaded African fertility fetish I'd tucked under my side of the mattress.

He was silent.

"You're the one who was talking about bad karma," I said.

"Yeah, well I just think strawberries and whipped cream might work better."

Even as I did all of this, I feared that I'd get what I wished for. On the days my writing was going well I didn't care if I ever got pregnant—I secretly hoped I wouldn't. After an evening with my three-year-old niece, who commanded me to sip from a play teacup, pretend the liquid burned me, and shriek, "Oh no!" until I thought I'd pass out from the tedium, I felt relieved not to have a child. On the way to a last-minute yoga class, I'd congratulate myself on the serenity and spontaneity of my life. Then each month when I got my period I cried.

I began surfing infertility Web sites, reading postings out loud to Steven. "Hey, hon, listen to this. It's from someone with the screen name Babyfever:

Bill's making me take a break! He says he's burnt out. He says that hopefully—*hopefully*—he'll be ready to reconsider in a couple of months. But only if I don't talk about getting pregnant. How will I get through it? Am I supposed to put on an act? Pretend to be a good wife and smile and be happy knowing I've had two miscarriages and now might never get pregnant? What if one of those months is the only one for the rest of my life when I can conceive?

I'm going to seduce him when I'm ovulating. He'll never know. Except that I haven't wanted to have regular sex in, like, a year.

"Man," I said. "That woman is out of control."

"I don't really need to hear that stuff," Steven said. I jumped up to hug him. "Don't worry," I promised. "I'll never be like that."

Five months. Then six. I made an appointment for Steven to have his sperm checked by a urologist, the first step in sussing out a potential problem. Up to 40 percent of infertility is what's called "male factor," (about the same percentage is female factor; the rest is unexplained) and it's the easiest glitch to identify. "There are only *men* here," he hissed, when we entered the waiting room. "Middle-aged and elderly men with *urological* problems. I don't even know what a urological problem is."

We were sent upstairs, where a nurse with a Russian accent handed Steven a cup and bellowed, "Take this down the hall and masturbate. Do not touch the inside of the cup."

Sadly, he didn't harbor any Nurse Ratchet fantasies. He slunk into a room that was bare except for a table and a towel-draped chair. "That towel made me think about all the other men who had sat there," he told me later. An array of magazines was scattered on the table: *Playboy*, *Penthouse*, the *Sports Illustrated* swimsuit issue, *Playgirl* (presumably for gay clientele), and, inexplicably, *Golf Digest*. "I tried to find something sexy, but I could hear the Russian nurse yelling outside, and people walking by. It was hard to find something . . . sustaining." He shook his head. "It wasn't my best work."

A few days later Steven's GP called with the preliminary results. His counts were low and too many of his sperm had damaged heads. "You're going to have a hard time getting pregnant," she said. That should've been devastating news, yet it left me weirdly chipper. If Steven was infertile, I could chalk childlessness up to fate. It was no one's fault—more specifically, it was not *my* fault. This had nothing to do with my age or how long I had waited to try to get pregnant. It wasn't retribution for my cavalier choices or my chronic ambivalence. I wasn't happy about the news, but I felt the weight of my own presumed guilt lift.

When we met with the urologist, though, he assured us that Steven's doctor had overreacted. "Steven doesn't have the fertility of a twenty-five-year-old, but he's still got plenty of decent sperm here." There should be enough, he said, more than enough, to knock a girl up.

"I'm worried about you getting pregnant," Steven said. We were driving across the Bay Bridge, on our way home from shopping in San Francisco. He'd been acting a little distant, a little stressed all afternoon. We were just gearing up for our seventh month of trying.

"Why?" I said.

"What if they're wrong? What if it gives you cancer again?"

I was stunned. We hardly talked about the cancer anymore. I hadn't stopped worrying about it; it was more that I couldn't allow myself the luxury of those fears. If I did, I might start agonizing over all sorts of things, like the ingredients in the toilet bowl cleaner or the noxious fumes from the cars backed up all around us on the bridge. I no longer fled the kitchen when the microwave was on. I'd stopped drinking carrot juice, which, antioxidants or no, I found repellant. I couldn't live that way.

Steven was staring straight ahead, his hands gripping the steering wheel. I reached over, hugged him as best I could across our seat belts. "I love you so much," I told him when I could speak again.

Can we talk about bad sex? My gynecologist, Risa Kagan, suggested a "postcoital test" before my next ovulation to see if my mucous was hostile to Steven's sperm. It was part of a basic fertility workup that also included blood tests to check my hormones, an ultrasound, and a form of medieval torture in which

28

blue dye was pumped through my remaining fallopian tube to see if it was clear. (It was.) "It's not like you're forty," Risa said when I went in to see her, "but time is of the essence here."

She told me to have intercourse immediately before my next appointment, which I shoehorned in after lunch during a busy week. Steven was running late and I was furious. He called me from the car to warn me that he didn't have much time. "Can you get started without me and be ready to go when I get there?" he asked.

Needless to say, neither of us was in the mood for love. "I feel like Risa is in bed with us," he complained. I glanced at the clock. "Just hurry up, will you? I'm going to miss the appointment." Luckily, Risa wasn't measuring the quality of our experience.

"Your mucous is gorgeous," she announced, stepping back from the microscope. (*Tell me something I don't know*, I thought.) A take-charge kind of gal herself with a brainy, East Coast style, Risa was part of a generation of women who had entered the field of medicine to change it, to be more of a partner than a parent to her patients. She seemed like a trusted older sister. She gestured for me to look through the lens. I could see Steven's sperm, brave sailors on a journey to nowhere, swimming with all their evolutionary might through a river of my exemplary fluid. Our horoscope signs may have clashed— I'm Sag, he's Pisces—but our love juices apparently got along fine. Good thing—the symbolism of my body rejecting Steven's sperm, refusing to make life with it, was too disturbing to consider.

* * *

Eight months. "This could be the problem," Risa said, tapping my chart. My labs had come back showing that the hormone progesterone was low during the second half of my cycle. "That would keep an embryo from implanting."

I asked her if that could be fixed.

She nodded. "You could try Clomid." Clomid was a fertility drug used for women who either didn't ovulate or, as in my case, didn't ovulate "robustly." I'd heard it was also implicated in ovarian cancer.

"Studies haven't supported that," Risa said, adding that she'd conceived her own second child on Clomid. "With my oldest, I'd gotten pregnant on the first try, so I assumed I'd have the second one exactly when I wanted. A year later, I could tell you exactly where I was every time I got my period. You know how it is. It's devastating. And in some ways, it's even harder when you already have a child, because you know what you're missing. It turned out that my progesterone levels were a little low. I didn't think twice about taking the Clomid, I wanted to get pregnant so badly. And whether it was the Clomid or not, I got pregnant the next month."

"Hmmm," I replied, noncommittal. I still wasn't eager to be part of what felt to me like a massive experiment in women's health. I wasn't *that* desperate to have a child, was I?

Risa continued talking. Clomid was a low-level intervention, a pill that I'd take only five days a month. It was inexpensive, too—only fifty dollars a cycle. Despite my reservations, I felt tempted. For the first time, I asked myself the Two Questions, the ones that would drive me for the next five years: What if this worked? What if it was the only way we could have a baby?

Risa scribbled a prescription and held it out to me. *I don't have to fill it*, I reasoned as I slipped it into my purse. *I'll just hang on to it, for insurance. What harm could that do?*

My left breast looked surprisingly good; the scar had faded quickly and the lumpectomy gave it a little midlife lift. But the radiation had killed the milk ducts, so it could never nourish a child. That's why, a week later, only my right breast felt like it was on fire, like it was being stung by scores of bees. I'd waited for my period to come, then waited some more.

"Would this be good news or bad news?" The checkout clerk at Long's Drug boomed as she rang up the home pregnancy test.

"Um, good, I think," I stammered, making a mental note not to get in her line if I ever bought hemorrhoid cream.

"Best of luck then," she said, grinning.

I shook the box, turned it round and round in my hands like it was a Magic 8 Ball. What if I were pregnant? What if I weren't? As long as I waited, I could remain comfortably in the hypothetical, my life wouldn't have to change. Finally, though, the suspense (and two cups of tea) got the better of me. Once again, I peed on a stick. Then I ran to my car, sped to Steven's office, and wordlessly held out the result. We gaped at each other for a good thirty seconds.

"You're pregnant?" he asked.

I plunked onto his lap, laughing, and threw my arms around him. Then we looked at each other again, our eyes wide. I felt like Dustin Hoffman and Katherine Ross in the final scene of *The Graduate*, staring slack-jawed out the back of a bus: we'd finally gotten what we thought we wanted. What now?

"You know, " Steven said, "I suddenly realize how much courage it takes to choose *not* to have children."

I could give a guided tour to all the places I've puked in Honolulu. Over there, by the band shell in Kapiolani Park. And at the curb next to the multiplex in Restaurant Row after suffering through the Robin Williams stinker *What Dreams May Come*. And oh yes, on the beach near where we once spotted Gwen Stefani. I was seven weeks pregnant when we left for our annual vacation. I vomited on the way to the airport. I vomited on the plane. I vomited out the window of the car on the way to the hotel and every couple of hours after that. In our favorite restaurants I cut my food into minuscule pieces and pushed it around the plate, even snuck some of it into my napkin hoping Steven wouldn't notice, would think I was having a grand time. I had no one to blame but myself; he'd offered to cancel the trip when the nausea set in, but I'd refused. I didn't want the baby already holding me back. The only thing that soothed me was the movement of the ocean. I floated over the reefs in my snorkel and fins, humming lullabies, imagining I was an embryo myself, rocking in a salty womb. I'd read somewhere that couples in which the man was at least ten years older than the woman were more likely to have sons—that was just about the distance between Steven and me. So I was sure the baby would be a boy. We'd already named him Kai, which means "ocean" in Hawaiian and Japanese.

Even the sea turned against me eventually, my stomach lurching with the waves. By the time we got back to Berkeley, I'd lost twelve pounds. Looking at my computer screen made me dizzy. I felt like such a wimp; women got pregnant all the time—what was wrong with me?

"This is not okay," Risa said when I went in for my first prenatal appointment. My blood pressure had plunged; I could hardly sit up. "You can't go on like this."

In some women, she explained, "morning sickness" spins out of control. No one knows why. Doctors used to be taught that it reflected a mother-to-be's ambivalence about the pregnancy. That, she added, was back when all obstetricians were male. A kinder interpretation says the nausea is a vestige of evolution, a biological alarm system designed to keep women from eating something that would harm the fetus during the initial, critical months. But that doesn't explain why some women don't have a lick of trouble while for others the illness itself becomes a threat to the pregnancy. Risa made arrangements for a nurse to come to my house with a temporary intravenous drip to stop me from dehydrating. "There is one good thing," she said. "Being so sick is usually a sign of a healthy pregnancy."

The next afternoon, Steven and I went to the hospital for a routine ultrasound and prenatal counseling. I was nearly eleven weeks pregnant, still feeling rocky, but full of confidence that all was well. The technician poured a cool, slippery, liquid onto my stomach. She ran the ultrasound wand over my belly, then left the room for a moment, returning with a long phallic device. I slid it inside of me and she scanned the screen again. "I think I'll get the doctor," she said, her voice neutral.

We knew. Steven took my hand, his lips compressed. I felt myself slipping into the familiar numbness of medical emergency. The doctor came in and broke the inevitable news—the fetus had stopped developing two weeks earlier. He ushered us to plastic chairs in the hallway while he called Risa's office.

"Are you relieved?" I asked Steven, thinking back to our *Graduate* moment.

"Maybe a little," he said. "Mostly, though, I'm sad."

We went through the rest mechanically. The D&C, the bleeding, telling our families and friends. My brother David had already told his children about their impending cousin. For the next year at unpredictable moments, like the middle of a Friday night dinner, my four-year-old niece would turn to me and say, "You lost your baby, didn't you, Aunt Peggy?" Each time felt like biting down on tin foil.

In the following weeks, Steven watched me closely for deeper signs of devastation. But honestly there weren't any, not then. I was sorry to lose the pregnancy, but I didn't have any difficulty sharing the excitement of two friends who were expecting babies the same week I had been due. I was happy for their happiness, ready to welcome the little lives they were creating. "I'm grateful that we got pregnant at all," I told Steven. "And we can start trying again in a month. If it happened once, that means it can happen again."

3

THE ONE THAT GOT AWAY

———— • ————

Larry Brown was my first true love. My junior high school notebooks are a mass of arrow-pierced hearts, our names entwined inside. "Larry + Peggy," "Larry & Peggy Brown," "Peggy Brown," "Dr. and Mrs. Larry Brown." There are two parallel smudges in the creamy paint on my parents' dining room wall where I propped my stockinged feet during the hours and years of our phone conversations, adolescent musings about poetry and God. We flirted and fought; he read me couplets from Ogden Nash and Shel Silverstein—not, perhaps, the most romantic of offerings—and I reciprocated with my own tortured verse. For years I sent his mom Mother's Day cards; I still confide in his dad.

As we got older, though, Larry grew more devout—or *frum* as it's called in Yiddish—and I less so, unable to reconcile Judaism with my incipient feminism. He stopped mixing milk and meat after his bar mitzvah; I converted to *Diet for a Small*

Planet vegetarianism. A few years later he rejected anything prepared in nonkosher cookware or served on *treif* plates, including those in his own mother's home. I stopped attending religious services. By our sophomore year of college he'd banished all shades of spiritual gray: if the Torah was God's word, how could he neglect any of its commandments? How could he pick and choose? Shared history, rather than shared belief or experience, kept our friendship afloat, though often just barely.

Shortly before graduation, Larry met Beth Karsh. He gushed to me about her intelligence, her compassion, her Jewish values. But there was a problem: he was about to go off to yeshiva in Israel for a semester before starting medical school in St. Louis; she had another year of undergraduate work to complete in Madison. Faced with the prospect of never seeing Beth again, Larry proposed. They'd been dating for just two months.

The following winter I flew in for their wedding from New York, where I'd moved after my own graduation. It was like being airlifted from the pages of *Bright Lights, Big City* into a Chaim Potok novel. A low wall, a *mechitzah*, ran the length of the sanctuary dividing the men from the women. The dancing at the reception was sex-segregated, too. On the men's side, one of Larry's friends performed Russian squat-kicks to klezmer music, jumping and twirling with a wine bottle balanced on his head. The women fanned out in front of Beth, skipping toward her and away, pretending to sweep the floor, to wash clothes, to rock a baby. I sat on the sidelines horrified. What kind of throwback had my friend become? The *mechitzah* wasn't the only thing separating us.

Their first baby was born a year later; the second, sixteen

months after that. I, meanwhile, was dating men with foreign accents, riding motorcycles, clubbing until dawn. By the time he finished his residency, Larry had five sons and three daughters; I'd long since lost track of their names. Once, when I'd worked up the courage to ask him how many children they planned to have, he'd replied, "As many as God gives us." To date, "God" (along with unprotected sex) had given them fifteen. That is not a misprint. Larry and Beth have fifteen children ranging in age from twenty years to nine months old. Larry and I no longer talked much, partly because a guy with fifteen kids doesn't have time for chitchat, and partly because there was too much tender territory between us. He disapproved of my marriage to a gentile, of the way I practiced (or didn't practice) Judaism. I was confounded by his fanaticism and the ever-growing family. Our relationship drifted, becoming little more than a party trick I would bring out to stun new friends. But Larry's mother had tipped him off: I was scheduled to give a talk in St. Louis that fall. He e-mailed me, inviting me to his home. I agreed right away; I missed him, missed the piece of my past he held, missed our rambling talks, our private jokes. I wondered whether underneath it all, the fundamentalist was still fundamentally himself.

I had found out about the miscarriage three days before the trip, but didn't consider canceling. I can't say why. Maybe I was still in shock, cruising along on autopilot. Maybe it was because as soon as the surgery was over, the nausea lifted and I felt more energetic than I had in weeks. Or maybe on some level I thought it would be therapeutic—Beth was my inverse, the woman I might have become if my life had gone differently.

After a few days hanging around her, I figured, I'd be relieved to be childless.

The main floor of the Browns' brick and clapboard house is a straight shot from the living room through the vestibule to the dining room. There are no rugs, no knickknacks, no coffee tables, no sharp corners. The most distinctive piece of furniture is a life-sized wooden sculpture of a zebra curled on the floor in front of the hearth. It was carved by Beth's stepfather. "That zebra is indestructible," Beth would tell me. "Larry can stand with his full weight on one of its ears."

Larry was still at work when I dropped by from my hotel the first evening. Beth was in the kitchen making grilled cheese sandwiches for the youngest eight children, slapping butter onto bread, peeling American cheese from a block of one hundred slices. She cooked them on her *milchig*, or dairy, stove. *Kashrut* demands complete separation of milk and meat, though the laws never say why. As practiced by the Browns, it requires not only two sets of utensils, dishes, and pots (one each for milk and meat) but also two ovens, two stovetops, two microwaves, two sinks, two sets of dish towels, and two dishwashers. They also have three refrigerators (one for holidays) and a deep freeze in the basement, though that's more to accommodate the sheer quantity of food they require than to satisfy any rules of ritual.

I had never felt comfortable with Beth—her choices, her lifestyle, were (I have to say it) inconceivable. Even the way she dressed freaked me out. She'd cut her hair short when she married, according to the customs of *tsnius*, or modesty, and covered it with a wig. She had three of them, each made of human hair and costing several thousand dollars; the one she wore today was a lustrous auburn, cut in layers that grazed her chin. I wouldn't have pegged it as a fake, except that occasionally when she scratched her head the whole thing moved. I'd never understood why a woman's own hair, no matter how frowsy, was considered alluring, but a beautifully coiffed wig wasn't—I guess the rabbis of yore didn't make provisions for feminine ingenuity. Beth even wore the wig, called a *sheitl*, when giving birth. Although it was unseasonably, uncomfortably hot, she also wore long sleeves and a skirt reaching her shins; thick, nylon knee-highs; and low-heeled pumps. (Men, too, are subject to laws of *tsnius*, though less stringently; the racks of Larry's closet were filled with identical white shirts and black pants. He doesn't wear shorts, and his sons aren't allowed to go shirtless, even in the house.)

My friends always assumed that Larry had "made" Beth have all these children, but that wasn't the case. He would've stopped earlier. Orthodox Jews can, in consultation with a rabbi, use birth control due to financial strain, overly close spacing of children, or to preserve the marriage. Beth and Larry could have claimed any of those pressures. Among other things, Beth developed gestational diabetes with several pregnancies and, unsurprisingly, had grown dangerously overweight. I had always figured that Larry and Beth were compensating for Larry's younger brothers and male friends who'd married gentiles, whose children (because Judaism is traditionally matrilineal) they didn't consider Jewish. But that wasn't it, either. They had so many children, Beth told me, because she wanted them.

Unlike Larry, Beth grew up in an Orthodox community. "When I was young I spent a lot of time at our rabbi's house," she said. "They had eleven kids. I liked the atmosphere there. I wanted a big family, too. And I'm excited every time I find out I'm pregnant. It never gets old. It's such a miracle. It's the same with the milestones; it was just as exciting when number fourteen took her first steps as it was when number one did."

I didn't know how to respond, I who wrestled with the decision to have even *one* child. But it didn't matter—with so many kids scampering in and out of the kitchen, banging into one another like bumper cars, further conversation was nearly impossible anyway. Nine-year-old Menashe, who wore a jersey emblazoned with the number ten (his place in the birth order) and—lucky for me—his name embroidered on his velvet yarmulke, had hitched a jump rope to a toddler ride-aboard and was pulling seven-year-old Gav through the house in a wild game of crack the whip. Four-year-old Noam was crying because they wouldn't include him. I glanced over Beth's shoulder and noticed Hadassah, twenty-three months, wielding a pizza cutter like a cutlass. A moment later I grabbed her as she toppled from a folding chair she was using to scale the kitchen counter, nearly tripping in the process over baby Ahuva, who was sucking her pacifier next to the stove. None of it fazed Beth. I had once read that parents of large families thrived on activity and unpredictability, yet I couldn't figure out how that jibed with Larry's and Beth's fixation on arcane rules about the blending of cotton and wool. I wondered if the mayhem was an antidote, a counterbalance to such hyperregulated lives.

"Dinner!" Beth called. Eight children thundered in, performed the blessing for washing their hands, said grace, and dug in to the sandwiches, a salad of prewashed lettuce, and bowls of homemade salmon chowder. A few minutes later Beth excused herself to sort through hand-me-downs with a friend, and sixteen eyes turned expectantly toward me. Noam, who was wearing a magician's cape, wanted to show me how he could pull a stuffed rabbit from a hat. Avishai, ten, wanted to describe in mind-numbing detail a roller coaster he once rode at Six Flags over St. Louis. Yonah, eleven, couldn't figure out how I knew their dad, since in his world boys aren't allowed to fraternize with girls. I tried to pay attention to all of them at once, to answer every question. Then Esther Neima, five, asked me how many children I had. I froze. "I have ten nieces and nephews," I fudged, pasting a smile on my face. My response satisfied her more than it did me.

Suddenly it seemed that coming here had been a mistake. I had to get away from all of those kids, at least for a minute. I asked Esther Neima to show me upstairs to the bathroom. After their eleventh child was born, the Browns had added a second story to their home with six bedrooms and three baths. The rooms were spare, not holding much more than a bunk bed and a desk. One of the boys' rooms had a computer (with no Internet access), another a drum set. No one had gotten around to putting anything on the walls, but streams of children's belongings—dirty clothes, water bottles, rollerblades—overflowed from each room, merged together in the central hallway. Esther Neima gave me a tour of the bathroom, pointing out the toilet, the sink, the soap.

She gestured to the door handle with a flourish. "And this," she said proudly, "is the lock."

By the time I collected myself and headed back downstairs, dinner was over, the kids scattered. Beth beckoned me into the living room, where she sat with three of the girls. Already I was adjusting to the distorted arithmetic of the Brown household; it felt like we were nearly alone. When I had left for the airport, Steven had told me to be sure to look in the Browns' cupboards. "How do people with fifteen kids get through the day?" he wondered. "Do they have gallon-sized peanut butter jars? Do they buy ketchup by the barrel?"

I was too dispirited to play Nancy Drew, but I did ask Beth for a few details. Every Brown child over the age of five had a job, she explained, such as setting the table, doing yard work, or taking out the garbage. Avishai packed all the lunches, though since that was one of the hardest tasks, he got summers and holidays off. Once they were twelve, they did their own laundry, too. Even so, keeping ahead of the clutter wasn't easy. "You can pick up fifteen times a day," Beth said. "You can wash thirty cups and two hours later there are thirty more."

The family has almost never eaten out, which, when you consider the number of years of incessant meal preparation, is mind-boggling. Even if they could afford it, there are no kosher restaurants in St. Louis. Beth pops by the grocery store for odds and ends at least once a day in her fifteen-seat van, the kind hotels use to chauffeur guests to and from the airport. She drives the kids to school, to synagogue, to orthodontist appointments, to piano lessons. And with all of that, she still feels guilty when she misses a Little League game. "All of the other parents are there," she said.

I smiled sympathetically, but I was actually thinking, *Please, God, get me back to my superficial, self-absorbed friends who spend all their time discussing which overpriced eatery makes the best anise crème brulée.*

Gav came running in. "Ima!" he shouted excitedly, using the Hebrew word for "mother." "Hadassah said my name! She said my name!" He picked up the baby, spun her around, planted a kiss on her cheek. "Ahuva! Hadassah said my name!" Gav beamed, the joy on his face so intense that I had to turn away.

Avishai came in to see what the racket was about and noticed my pained expression. "Are you enjoying St. Louis?" he asked. "Or is there too much talking?"

I didn't connect with Larry until the next morning. He called my hotel at 10:30, his voice still thick with sleep. "What are you doing?" he asked.

"I just got back from Starbucks."

"I'm jealous." He'd gotten home from his sixteen-hour work-day at eight o'clock that morning, sat in a chair next to the din-ing table, and, he said, "That's the last thing I remember." His two-and-a-half-hour siesta would be his sleep for the day; he was about to say his morning prayers, then wanted to get to-gether. "I average fifteen or twenty hours of sleep—a week."

"You realize," I replied, "that would be considered a form of torture in most places."

Larry was an emergency room doctor, working full-time in two different hospitals, often doing back-to-back shifts. Beth, meanwhile, was the principal of secular education at their kids' Jewish day school. Most of her compensation came by way of free tuition, which at ninety-six hundred dollars a year for nine years for fifteen kids (plus summer camp) is an impressive sum. In actual cash, though, she made less than Roberta, the two youngest girls' nanny.

By the time I walked over to the house, Beth had been gone for hours. She'd woken at five, slapped together two pans of lasagna and four loaves of garlic bread for dinner, driven the older boys to the synagogue for their morning prayers, then come home to prepare for a meeting. The older children dressed the younger ones and set them up with Cap'n Crunch and Golden Grahams (sugary cereals and junk food are almost universally kosher). By 7:45 they'd piled into the van and left.

Larry greeted me by taking a step back and clasping his hands behind him. Death is considered impure in traditional Judaism, and since menstruation represents the monthly loss of potential life, so is a woman having her period, or one who hasn't subsequently dunked herself in the ritual bath. Since it would be rude to ask, Orthodox men err on the side of caution. They don't touch women other than their wives and daughters. I was still bleeding from my miscarriage; I couldn't imagine in this fragile state suffering the added insult of being forbidden to embrace my husband, to seek the comfort of his arms. Still, when Larry grinned and said, "The hug is implied," I couldn't help but smile back, duly disarmed.

It had been nearly ten years since we'd seen each other. He was thicker around the middle than I remembered, the curl cropped out of his hair, which, like his beard, was graying. But he had the same glinting brown eyes, the same amused smile of the boy I'd known—the one who'd once snuck a stack of LPs into Junior Congregation, slipping one under his tush each time we rose in prayer, then, his gaze piously innocent, plopping down to break it with a rude crack.

While Larry made coffee, I worked up the energy to snoop, convincing myself it was on Steven's behalf. The Browns' pantries were surprisingly lightly stocked, all things considered. There were a few industrial-sized items—cardboard boxes filled with packages of cookies or mac & cheese, a few jumbo jars of Jif, and some tubs of salad dressing—but most things were the same size and quantity as the ones I bought. "I'd buy more in bulk if it were up to me," Larry explained, "but I'm not around enough. Beth is efficient, but she isn't necessarily organized. So she'll go to the grocery store three times in a day. And she has something like ten sets of keys, because she can never remember where she's left them; that way she'll happen across one if she needs it. I think she kind of has to be that way, though. Whenever she's doing something, she's interrupted. So she does what's in front of her, and if she has to stop in the middle and start something else, she just does that."

According to the *Guinness Book of World Records*, Beth and Larry are amateurs. The greatest officially recorded number of children born to one mother is—wait for it—sixty-nine. Here's the kicker: no one remembers the woman's name. She's gone down in history as "the first wife of one Feodor Vassilyev," an eighteenth-century Russian peasant. That nameless woman had twenty-seven births, including sixteen pairs of twins, seven sets of triplets, and four sets of quads. By the time she was done, she probably didn't remember her own name.

I knew that five-and-a-half dozen children was hardly comparable to one or two, but that story only reinforced my suspicion that motherhood made women disappear. "People with no kids think this is chaos," Larry said. I didn't disagree. "But it's more settled than you think. Dressing or feeding two or three is hard, it's relentless. But in a way we have more independence, because the older ones can change diapers, carry the babies—we have more help in the house than most people."

"Even so," I said, "the time, the energy—how do you even manage to make any more children?"

"It only takes fifteen times to have fifteen kids."

"Seriously, Larry."

"Seriously," he repeated. "That's not much of an exaggeration. We are *very* fertile." *And I'm not*, I thought, imagining how much harder that would be to endure if I were part of Larry's community.

I followed Larry to his basement office, which doubled as a storage space for bicycles. The shelves were stuffed with family photos; Hebrew texts; his old, beloved volumes of Nash and Silverstein; and a few contemporary best sellers. A collage he'd made to announce Beth's eleventh pregnancy to his parents hung above his desk: rows of head shots of the ten existing kids followed by a sonogram. Larry's parents, I knew, cringed at the news of each new grandchild, though over the years they'd developed a grudging tolerance. Occasionally, when I visited them in Minneapolis, one of them would joke, "It's a good thing *you* didn't marry Larry," and we'd all laugh. Somewhere in their voices, though, was a hint of wistfulness. Maybe if Larry and I had wed, we would have moderated each other, met in the middle rather than spinning out to our respective religious extremes. Maybe by now we'd be a nice Jewish couple, living in a Midwestern suburb providing our parents with a socially acceptable three or four grandchildren. It was a comfortable dream, so much simpler than the path I'd followed—I sometimes mourned its loss myself—but it wasn't ours.

I've always loved spending time with Larry's parents. After nearly fifty years together, they are still affectionate, still enjoy each other's company. They read the same books, travel, and attend concerts and theater. My parents are much the same, and that deep rapport was what I'd hoped for, what I cherished in my relationship with Steven. I would gladly sacrifice parenthood, I thought, before giving up any of that. Larry's priorities were different. "Beth and I have never spent much time together," he admitted. "We hardly saw each other before we were married, and then we had Yossi so soon after. I've asked her, 'When the kids move out and we sit down to dinner, will we have anything to talk about?'"

"But don't you miss that time?" I asked. "Wasn't that what you expected?"

He shrugged. "You can only feel the loss of something you've had."

"I just don't get it," I pushed. "You work eighty hours a week. You don't see your wife and kids. You don't take vacations. You don't even sleep. What kind of quality of life is that?"

Larry nodded, leaning back in his char. "Two things give me pause about everything. Time and money. I use all the time I have and I'm still always behind with everything. Whenever I do one thing there's an accounting of what I'm *not* doing." He pointed to a broken electrical plate against the wall. "So am I going to fix someone's bike, or fix that electrical plate? Am I going to clean and straighten, which could be a full-time job in this house, or am I going to take the kids to the library?

"And money. I have no idea how much it costs to keep this family afloat, but it's definitely more than I make. But what is financial strain? We can still pay for clothes, for food. We could move to a smaller house, with three kids to a room. Stress is in the eye of the beholder."

"You know that sounds insane," I said.

"I know it does to you, yes," he said. "But part of this for me is realizing we're not in control of everything. Some people don't use contraception and have no kids at all or, unfortunately, have difficulty." I smiled weakly. "Other people have two children or six. If we have fifteen children, that's what's supposed to happen.

"And I like everything I do," he added. "I like the kids. I like my job. By Tuesday I've worked as much as some people work in a whole week, but I never feel like I don't want to be doing it. Everything is a gift from God, everything. To an outsider this all can look like a burden. But tomorrow I could have a stroke. I could have an accident. I could lose my wife, my house, my kids. So I work hard. But everything I do I find precious."

Suddenly, Larry leapt up. "I almost forgot," he said, and pulled out a volume by British poet Robert Service from his shelf. "Listen to this." He read "My Prisoner," about a World War I Tommy's encounter with a German soldier, in a full-on cockney accent. "Isn't that brilliant?" he asked, and without waiting for a response, launched into a second poem, "The Ballad of Sam McGee." The swashbuckling saga wasn't something I would've picked but Larry was so jazzed to share it with me. Every few lines, he would glance up eagerly, eyes shining, voice rising. Almost unconsciously, I slipped off my shoes. As I propped up my stockinged feet, I listened to my friend—I tried to hear what he was hearing.

A poster of the poem *"Eishet Chayil"* ("A Woman of Valor") hangs framed on the wall of the Browns' living room. *A woman of valor, who can find?* it begins. *Her worth is far beyond that of rubies.* It's the traditional serenade by a groom to his bride, the song a husband sings to praise his wife at the Sabbath table. Most Jews I knew had dropped the custom long ago, considering it demeaning. It's true, the *Eishet Chayil* is the original woman who does too much, staying up deep into the night and rising while it's still dark to do for her family, denying her own needs, seeking no glory. On the other hand, our Ms. *Chayil* earns her own living selling cloth, farming, or acquiring real estate. She manages a household staff, gives to the needy, serves God. Rather than her looks, she's cherished for her integrity, dignity, and wisdom. I'd always suspected the *Eishet Chayil* model was part of the reason that so many feminist leaders were Jews, from Betty Freidan to Gloria Steinem to Susan Faludi to Rebecca Walker.

If *"Eishet Chayil"* has ever come to life, though, it is in the person of Beth Brown. Shortly before my visit, a pregnant friend of hers with six children went on bed rest; Beth moved the woman's entire family into her home for two weeks. This on top of her own fifteen children and full-time job. And I didn't hear about it from her—Larry told me. To her it wasn't a big deal: "I enjoy having a lot of people around" was all she would say. "There's always something happening." When I'd suggested that was what most people would *dislike* about it, Beth had only smiled. "It's not an imposition," she had insisted. "If our kids get sick, people are there for us, too. That's just how it works."

How, exactly, did it work for me? If Beth was a righteous woman, what was I? My own sense of obligation seemed shallow by comparison. Although I'd like to be the sort who whips up meals for sick friends, I rarely followed through, pleading the excuse of a busy life. Even at my most generous, I wouldn't move someone else's family into my home. Nor did I expect much from anyone else beyond Steven; I usually considered that to be a mark of self-sufficiency. Watching Beth, though, I began to wonder where—without children, without community—I truly belonged.

Back in my hotel room, I flipped on the TV to a flickering image of Kelly McGillis in a white lace snood. The film was *Witness*, the romantic thriller in which a cop played by Harrison Ford is forced to hide out among the Amish. Eventually, his derision is overcome by their simplicity and caring, he recognizes the soullessness of contemporary life. "I'm right there with you, Harrison," I said to the screen.

Larry was wrong. I think you can feel the loss of something you've never had, or at least a phantom longing for it. I'd never had faith; it had sometimes buzzed toward me, as improbable as a hummingbird, only to retreat when I reached for it. Mine is a messy, inconsistent philosophy, one that is dominated by the shades of gray Larry shunned: the gun metal of agnosticism, the storm clouds of contradiction, the dove breast of ambivalence. How reassuring it must be to know precisely what was expected of you, to be free from the uncertainties of finding your own way. How consoling to feel that your miscarriage, or your infertility, or your fifteen children were God's will. I could never do it, but sometimes I dearly wished I could.

Beth and I were repelling magnets. I was no *Eishet Chayil* and she was no feminist—she didn't even expect her daughters to go to college. I would never want her life, was grateful to live in a time when it wasn't forced upon me, and yet, to my surprise, part of me was jealous of her. Somehow she'd managed to "have it all": a respected career, a loving husband, a warm family, a supportive community. Happiness. Could I say the same about myself?

"So can you recite their names and birthdays?" I asked Larry. It was almost dinner time again. He'd just popped the lasagna and garlic bread into the oven and was pouring lettuce out of a bag, chopping up cucumbers for a salad. A cluster of the boys were doing gymnastics on the kitchen floor, Menashe dangling upside down from twelve-year-old Akiva's waist, Noam swinging from his back.

"Yeah, I can," Larry said, laughing. "But when they page me at work I have them punch in their number in the birth order. Otherwise, whoever answers the phone when I call back asks the first five people he sees if they'd called me and I eventually get tired of waiting."

He moved on to a pile of dishes in the sink. My secular friends would be envious; their purportedly egalitarian husbands don't do half of what Larry does around the house and they have twice as much time. In addition to laundry and dishes, Larry mops the floors and does all the mending. ("Beth has never sewn on a button," he boasted.) Every Friday afternoon, he gets down on his hands and knees and scrubs six bathroom floors to prepare for Shabbos. That domestic competence predated his piety—credit his mother, who made sure her three boys pitched in at home. At any rate, equality in housework is one thing; in the House of God it's another. Larry's daughters don't attend yeshiva. They can't study Talmud, can't hold positions of leadership at the synagogue, can't become rabbis or cantors. Beth's authority at school stops at the door of the Hebrew classrooms. Women have fewer *mitzvot*, or commandments, to fulfill, too (supposedly because they'd conflict with the higher calling of household responsibilities). That's why Orthodox men will tell you they thank God each morning for not making them female.

"What you don't understand is that we may have different roles for men and women, but the wife is not *inferior*," Larry told me. "Beth is not inferior. It's a distortion of American culture to think that the person who has the greatest influence on a child's values and development is inferior to the one who brings in the money. Men may have imposed that ideology, but the women who didn't glorify the domestic role contributed to it, too."

I flinched; I'd been one of those renegade women and secretly feared my miscarriage was retribution. At the same time, Larry's perspective seemed as skewed as my own. Separate could never be equal when one half of the equation was economically dependent on the other. Housework would never be valued until men participated in it fully. I doubted that transformation was possible in a community so invested in differences.

As a treat, Beth had arranged for the kids to swim at a friend's house, but since her nephew, Sha'uli, was visiting—and *tsnius* prohibited the Browns from seeing members of the opposite sex, aside from parents and siblings, in bathing suits—the girls were going to one pool with her and the boys to another with Larry. She explained this to me so deftly that it wasn't until later I realized Sha'uli wasn't the only concern: the Brown males couldn't see *me* in a bathing suit, either.

I hadn't brought one anyway, so I only dangled my legs in the water. In capris and a tank top, though, I was still flashing more skin than Beth. On the off chance that the husband of the couple who owned the pool might come home and catch a glimpse of her, she swam in her *sheitl*, a calf-length skirt, and an enormous T-shirt which read, "Who Are All These Kids and Why Are They Calling Me Mom?" Of all of the customs I witnessed at the Browns, *tsnius* rankled me most. Nineteen-year-old Shira worked out on the treadmill in the basement wearing an ankle-length skirt and long sleeves. Even five-year-old Esther Neima covered up. "We're taught that what's important is the inside of a person," Larry had told me. "So the idea is not to advertise your body. You shouldn't neglect the outside, but if you dress to call attention only to your physicality, what does that mean?" I got the point, but to me it seemed that *tsnius*, like the Muslim practice of *purdah*, could be too easily manipulated to silence women, to bar us from public places, to force the shrouding of ankles and eyes.

A bank of thunderheads rolled in. I shifted to a lounge chair under the eaves where I wouldn't get wet. I watched Beth shushing and coaxing, playing with and reprimanding the six children who were with us. The rising humidity made her seem far away, as if she were behind glass. I had come to respect Beth, but I'd never be at ease with her. I'd always be comparing us, wondering what it would be like to be her, flirting with the possibility then rejecting it. And I'd never really understand.

We drove home in silence. I couldn't tell if she noticed or cared that we'd run out of things to say. I sensed, though, that she was weary of my presence. Maybe that was just me—the novelty of being around fifteen children and hundreds of arbitrary rules was beginning to wear thin. Beth flipped on a cassette of religious-themed doo-wop songs. All of the tapes in her car featured men's voices; women's are considered too licentious for male ears.

> *Rebbe tried to teach us Torah each and every day*
> *We just closed our eyes and ears to what he had to say*
> *Every afternoon we'd sit and watch our TV sets*
> *Talking about the Yankees, the Dodgers, and the Mets*

Harrison Ford be damned—I wanted to return to the twenty-first century.

By 10:30 I couldn't stifle my yawns. Beth noticed and offered to drive me back to my hotel. She had to go to the grocery store anyway to buy a thank-you balloon for the couple whose pool we'd used. She wanted to have it waiting at their kosher butcher shop when they arrived for work the next morning. There was still a sink full of dishes to wash, bills to pay, and boxes of trash and recycling to drag to the curb. Larry had to be at work by seven the next morning to start another sixteen-hour day. Even so, he offered to drive me to the airport.

"My flight takes off at six A.M.," I said, shaking my head.

"That's okay," he said. "When do you want to leave your hotel?"

Hadassah tugged on my pants leg and I hoisted her in my arms. With her dark eyes and blonde Shirley Temple curls, she resembled the daughter I imagined Larry and I would have had if we'd married. He had noticed, too. "If I couldn't prove that Beth was her mother," he cracked, "I'd be suspicious."

I held her closer, had a wild urge to cut and run. *It's not fair*, I thought. Larry had fifteen children; why couldn't I even have one? If I had done the "right" thing, followed the proscribed path, would I be a mother now? Hadassah began to squirm. I tousled her curls and—though it ripped my heart out to do it—handed her to her father. We weren't in high school anymore; I'd made my choices.

"Larry," I said, as I turned away. "Do me a favor. Sleep the extra hour tomorrow instead of driving me. Consider it my gift to you."

I came home from the airport to a message from Risa, who'd called to fill me in on the pathology report from the miscarriage. "You are the last woman I want to have to tell this," she said when we spoke. "You had something called a partial molar pregnancy."

"A what?"

"It happens in about one in every thousand pregnancies," she explained. "It's a condition in which two sperm fertilize an egg." *Hmm*, I thought: *Steven must've been overcompensating for that insulting semen analysis*. Rather than twins, Risa continued, a fetus with too many chromosomes to survive is created as well as abnormal cells in the placenta. If any of those cells remained after the D&C, they could implant, turning into tumors that could spread and, without chemotherapy, eventually be deadly.

It was a pregnancy that could turn into cancer. Who had ever heard of such a thing? "What are the chances that will happen?" I asked.

"I don't know. In a full molar pregnancy the chances are about one in five. It's not clear with a partial molar. But the way we tell is by drawing your blood every week and checking for a rise in the pregnancy hormone. If it goes up and you're not pregnant, something's wrong."

"But what if I *am* pregnant?"

She paused. "I'm sorry. You have to use contraception for a while. If you got pregnant there'd be no way to tell if you had a tumor. And if you did develop a tumor it would be dangerous to the baby."

I could barely speak. "How long do I have to wait?"

She paused again. "I'm going to do some research. Normally it's a year, but maybe it doesn't have to be that long. At least six months."

Six months? A year? I thought about Larry and Beth—no way could this be God's will.

"Do you want to know the sex?" Risa asked before hanging up.

"No," I said evenly, though I felt like howling. "I don't think so."

When I told Steven the news, he wrapped his arms around me. He wasn't worried, he said. "Even if we have to wait for a year to try again, that's twelve extra months that we can enjoy being together, that we can do fun things as a couple."

I buried my face in his neck and cried, newly grateful, after my visit to the Browns, for his touch. I felt like the luckiest unlucky woman in the world.

4

HOOKED

———— ∙ ————

Clomid was my gateway drug: the one you take because, *Why not—everyone's doing it*. Just five tiny pills. They'll give you a boost, maybe get you where you need to go. It's true, some women can stop there. For others, Clomid becomes infertility's version of *Reefer Madness*. First you smoke a little grass, then you're selling your body on a street corner for crack. First you pop a little Clomid, suddenly you're taking out a second mortgage for another round of in vitro fertilization (IVF). You've become hope's bitch, willing to destroy your career, your marriage, your self-respect for another taste of its seductive high. *Here are your eggs. Here are your eggs on Clomid. Get the picture?*

It was nine months before Risa gave us the nod to resume baby making. Rather than gestate a child during that time, I had dusted off my diaphragm and submitted to weekly blood tests to make sure my hormones weren't running amok. Aside from that regular reminder that my freaky pregnancy was trying to kill me, there was a certain reprieve in the enforced break. My life, and our marriage, expanded again beyond my ovulation cycle. We made love more, laughed more, fought less. I began to believe, as I once had, that I'd be okay no matter what happened.

That dream was short-lived. In three rounds of trying, my progesterone was low twice. By now I was thirty-seven. Thirty-seven and a half, actually. For the first time since I was five, half birthdays mattered. I wasn't infertile, not technically. The official definition of infertility is twelve months of unprotected sex without a pregnancy. I'd gotten pregnant in eight. I was, however, in a time crunch. We could keep going and hope for the best, but infertility drugs become less effective as a woman ages. If I held off much longer, I might pass the point where they could help me. So which was wiser—to put my faith in my body or in science?

Clomid works by tricking your brain into thinking it's not making enough estrogen during the first half of your cycle. That puts into overdrive two other among the alphabet soup of female hormones—follicle stimulating hormone (FSH) and luteinizing hormone (LH), both of which affect egg development—creating bigger, better ovulations. Nearly half of women who try it get pregnant, most within three months. Those seemed like pretty sweet odds. The trade-offs can be hot flashes, blurred vision, "emotional side effects," and—be careful what you wish for—twins. In some women Clomid can also dry up cervical mucous, blocking rather than promoting pregnancy, which meant I'd clock even more time in the bathroom poking at myself to be sure the juices were flowing.

"I thought you said that drug caused ovarian cancer," Steven remarked.

"I said it raises the risk, but only if you take it for more than a year," I said, more blithely than I felt. "No one does that anymore. The longest I'd do it would be six months."

I didn't tell him the other part—that Clomid also appears to increase the cancer risk for women who never ultimately bear a child, though it's not clear whether it's the drug or the infertility itself that's the culprit. *No problem*, I thought, *it just has to work.*

Talk about ratcheting up the stakes. Swallowing that little white pill was the first time I did something I swore I wouldn't in order to get pregnant: I willingly put my health on the line. It was in that moment that desire and denial merged to become obsession; it was then, right then, that doing anything to get pregnant, regardless of the consequences, became possible.

"You're trying to control me!" Steven yelled.

"I am not!" I said.

"Yes you are!" He'd been pedaling his exercise bicycle in our den, something he did for a half hour each day. Now he swiveled to face me. "First you told me no jockey shorts," he said, enumerating on his fingers.

"You never wore jockey shorts," I interrupted.

"Still, you said it. Then you said no hot baths."

"You're not supposed to heat up your testicles. Hot baths kill sperm for three months."

"Men in Japan take hot baths every day. If that were true there'd be no Japanese children."

"They don't have borderline sperm."

"The doctor said my sperm was fine. Now every time you

walk by this room you look at me like I'm killing our chance to have a baby."

"It's proven that men who ride bicycles have lower sperm counts," I said, my voice shaking with anger. "You know that. And you're deliberately riding that bike. I'm taking a pill that's doing God knows what to my body so that we can have a child, and you can't even give up that fucking bike for a few months."

"Then come to me like a person and talk to me about it instead of giving me your little looks. I am not doing this to hurt you. And anyway, it isn't going to make any difference."

"It *will!*"

"You're being ridiculous. If you don't stop this, I'm not having fertility sex this month."

The Web posting from Babyfever that I'd dismissed—and the easy promise I'd made to Steven after reading it—flashed through my mind. I ignored it. "You cannot ride that bike! You cannot ride that bike! *You cannot ride that bike!*" I shouted.

Never mind cancer. Clomid's hormones made me a raving lunatic. I may have been right about the bike's lowering sperm count—it does, really—but lately my response to any challenge, no matter how small, was rage. The way Steven chewed his toast in the morning infuriated me. When he commented on a sloppily folded T-shirt, I dumped a basket of laundry on him. The okra he put in the minestrone was an obvious affront. (He knew I hated okra.) My hostility peaked around ovulation. "Why don't you just get a porn video and watch it in the other room," I said. "When you're ready, I'll be in bed."

"It's really better if you're interested, too."

I shrugged. "Yeah. Well, wake me up if I'm sleeping."

A few weeks later, he gave away the exercise bike.

Another three months went by. My progesterone was pumping. My mucous was gorgeous. We had the timing right. Still, nothing happened. Risa recommended we add intrauterine insemination (IUI) to the Clomid using Steven's sperm. He would once again get busy with a Dixie cup, then she'd inject his boys directly into my uterus, giving them a running start. The cost would still be minimal, about $350 a month. But we'd crossed another critical threshold: sex—or at least intercourse—was no longer a precondition of conception. We'd become a threesome, though not the fun kind. I lay on an exam table, shivering in my snowflake-covered hospital gown, legs in stirrups. Steven stood by my head, where I could focus on his face, holding my hand. Risa threaded a slim plastic tube through my cervix. It cramped a little. Afterward I stayed prone for fifteen minutes, my tush propped on a cushion. Steven kissed me, but I couldn't shake the idea that Dr. Kagan might have just fathered my child.

My thirty-eighth birthday came and went. "I'm aggressive with this in your age group," Risa said. "You need to think about a specialist." She gave me the number of a local guy. "He's one of the best in the Bay Area. Maybe you won't need him. You've only tried Clomid four times. But he's booked months in advance. If you make the appointment, you'll have it just in case.

"If anyone can get you pregnant," she added, "he can."

Gee, I thought. *And I was hoping Steven would.*

* * *

The descent into the world of infertility is incremental. Those early steps seem innocuous, even quaint; IUI was hardly more complex than using a turkey baster. You're not aware of how subtly alienated you become from your body, how inured to its medicalization. You don't notice your motivation distorting, how conception rather than parenthood becomes the goal, how invested you become in its "achievement." Each decision to go a little further seems logical. More than that, it begins to feel inevitable. My hesitations about motherhood hadn't disappeared, but they were steamrolled by my drive to succeed at pregnancy.

By our last round of Clomid we'd completely mechanized the attempt to conceive. The drug controlled the development of my follicle, the fluid-filled sac that contained a microscopic egg. Risa measured it every few days with an ultrasound. When it was ripe, a nurse injected me with a hormone that triggered ovulation. Twenty-four hours later Steven would visit the Russian nurse, where, after a stint with *Golf Digest*, his sperm was washed and spun, the Olympic contenders separated from those doing the dog paddle. That was my cue: I tucked the vial of his best stuff inside my bra (now the most erotic part of the process) to keep it warm while we race-walked out of the lab, past the Whole Foods and the Chevron station (at which point I clapped my hands across my chest, to protect our future progeny from any toxic fumes), up the stairs of Risa's building, and into an exam room, where she transferred the contents to my uterus. My hormones were kicking. Steven's sperm was turbocharged. I didn't get pregnant.

It is one thing, I was discovering, to think, "Maybe I won't have kids," and quite another to be told, "Maybe you can't." This is how impatience turns to desperation.

Hope? Dr. Aleksandr Stawecki's waiting room was steeped in it, right down to the blue and rose furniture reminiscent of a nursery. A sculpture of an expectant mother, hand curled around her belly, stood on a table in one corner. To its right were educational pamphlets on fertility drugs, IVF, and egg donation. To its left was a shelf of three-ring binders bursting with birth announcements and holiday cards from satisfied customers: other people's memories that we wished for our own. There was a picture of a laughing family posed with a snowman, of a baby cast as Jesus in a Nativity scene, of twin boys with the peeling, freckled noses of summer.

You couldn't help but project yourself into those albums. Once you did, once you envisioned yourself wreathed in the smug victory of parenthood, how could you retain your objectivity? The message was clear. Science could relieve our pain. Science, in the form of the good doctor, would deliver our baby to us. What empty hand wouldn't grasp at that straw?

Dr. Stawecki came out to greet us, an Eastern European man whose ring of white hair, white beard, and white jacket suggested both a guru's wisdom and a physician's expertise. "He looks like Oliver Sacks," Steven whispered to me as we followed him to his office.

"I think he looks like God," I whispered back.

The doctor had a reputation among his patients for being gruff, even rude. It's true, he wasn't warm. But we appreciated his bluntness—it won our trust. According to him, our main problem was that I was thirty-eight (and a quarter). "A woman's age is the greatest determinant of a successful pregnancy both for IVF and spontaneous conception," he explained, in his clipped accent. "You're born with all of your eggs, and they age with the rest of the organism. As they do, there are more errors in the chromosomes, and the embryos derived from those defective eggs ultimately won't be successful in implanting a healthy pregnancy. We know it's the eggs, because with donor eggs the age of the recipient has little impact on the likelihood of conception."

He pulled out a graph to illustrate his point. It showed a gentle downward slope in the rates of healthy pregnancy between ages eighteen and thirty-five then—*Whammo!* The bough breaks, the cradle falls, and down come your dreams of baby and all. "The biological clock truly starts ticking at thirty-three," he added. "It gets louder and louder at thirty-five, and by forty-five it's stopped."

Steven looked stricken. He traced the line with his finger. "I always thought it was a gradual decline, but it's like falling off a cliff." He turned to me. "Did you know this?"

"Kind of," I said, feebly. "I thought if we started at thirty-five we'd probably be fine." The truth was, I'd never seen it laid out quite so starkly. Women's magazines warned that fertility slips away with age, but I armored myself against the message by looking at it politically. The "infertility crisis" sounded to me like the "man shortage" of the mid-1980s, the one that claimed a woman who wasn't married by forty was more likely to be killed by a terrorist than to catch a husband. That was not only wrong, but inverted—there was actually a glut of single *men* on the market. Besides, although one out of three women over thirty-five may have trouble getting pregnant, the other two won't. I'd written the issue off as another attempt to scare women back to the kitchen.

Steven was staring at the chart again. "It's like our chances are disappearing by the minute," he said, softly.

"Yes," Dr. Stawecki agreed, seeming oblivious to our dismay. He pulled out another piece of paper and a pen. "Your cycle is about thirty-four days," he said to me. "Given your track record, I calculate the odds that you'll conceive on your own as"—he paused a moment—"less than ten percent."

"But," I corrected, "I did get pregnant."

"A pregnancy with a miscarriage is not the proper end point for fertility. It doesn't solve the problem."

I nodded, chastened by my own failure.

"If we add injectible medications with intrauterine insemination, your chances would increase to about . . . fifteen percent a cycle."

Steven winced.

"With in vitro fertilization," Dr. Stawecki paused again, "the odds are closer to thirty percent."

Thirty percent? Coming in here, those odds would've made me blanch—the likelihood was 70 percent that we *wouldn't* have a baby—but suddenly they sounded pretty good.

"One in three?" Steven said. "That's not so terrible."

I didn't know anyone (other than Risa) who'd conceived using fertility drugs alone, but my sister-in-law had gotten pregnant twice using a less invasive cousin of IVF; several other friends had, too. Maybe we would be like them. Steven felt optimistic. I was guilt-ridden. We were sold.

Walking back down the hallway, I stopped in front of a framed list of the names of all the babies that the doctor had made. I wondered how soon our child's name would be up there. I wasn't euphoric exactly, but I was heartened. We were finally getting the help we needed. Dr. Stawecki and his team would take the guesswork, the agony, out of getting pregnant. All we had to do was follow their instructions.

In IVF a woman injects herself with hormones to stimulate the development of multiple eggs—the more the merrier. When mature, they're surgically removed and placed in a petri dish with her husband's sperm (*in vitro* is Latin for "in glass"). In that unnatural environment they're supposed to do what comes naturally—form embryos. After incubating for a few days, several of the best looking—those with the most symmetrical cells that are dividing the fastest—are transferred back to the woman's womb. One or two for a younger, more fertile woman; three or four for a doddering oldster like me; eight for those people who believe it's God's will that they end up with quintuplets (though, strangely, not God's will that they accept their infertility).

No one knows exactly what makes the next part work, but a couple of weeks later—Hocus Pocus Jiminy Crocus—with any good luck, you've made a baby. A single cycle costs about twelve thousand dollars, none of which is covered by insurance. That put us in the class of people for whom having a baby depended on having the means. One of Steven's friends had opted against IVF for that reason. She and her husband could afford either one round of IVF or adoption, but not both. Adoption guaranteed them a child. Over time I would almost envy the clarity imposed by their financial limits. I knew women who'd gone through six, even seven rounds of IVF, sometimes traveling to another state to go to a new clinic that offered a different protocol. There would always be a next new thing to try. And as long as the money holds out and there's a possibility, a sliver of a chance, that you could bear a child yourself, it's excruciating to turn away.

So twelve thousand dollars on a 30-percent shot at success—it seemed to me that only a sucker would take that bet. Except that the potential jackpot was so great. And, again, there were those two nagging questions. *What if it works?* I thought, as I wrote the first of many checks to the clinic. *What if this is the only way we can have a child?*

For nearly two weeks I injected myself with the purified urine of postmenopausal Italian nuns—that's what the first drug prescribed to me was originally made of. Why Italian? I don't know. Why nuns? Postmenopausal women produce massive amounts of the hormone that stimulates egg growth in a futile attempt to revive the ovaries. They excrete the overrun in their pee. Retirement convents offer the most efficient one-stop shopping for elderly women (though I can't quite picture how they gather the goods). We get pregnant, they get enough money for a new stained-glass window. Everyone wins. It certainly put a new spin on the notion of Immaculate Conception: my potential child would be conceived without intercourse via an egg created by a virgin's pee. Putting voodoo dolls beneath my mattress no longer seemed so unreasonable.

My second drug was equally bizarre, derived from the ovaries of Chinese hamsters. Why Chinese? Again, no clue, though I hoped the drug wouldn't hold a grudge against Steven's Japanese sperm. Neither nun pee nor hamster ovaries came cheap: three vials injected morning and evening plus another drug to suppress my natural cycle ran over $350 a day—the same as I'd spent in an entire month doing IUI with Risa. A girl could buy a lot of shoes with that kind of scratch.

In addition to the familiar side effects of Clomid, the injectible drugs bumped up the likelihood of twins or triplets to 30 percent. That gave us pause. On one hand, it would be a bargain: two for the price of one, an instant family. Steven, whose siblings were each about a year apart, sort of liked the idea of our kids being the same age. On the other hand, he also recalled seeing a friend six months after becoming the father of twins: "They had extinguished the light from his eyes," Steven said. "He looked like a well-dressed character from *Night of the Living Dead*." In the end we convinced ourselves that while we would surely be among the 30 percent who succeeded in getting pregnant, we wouldn't be in the 30 percent of that group who had twins. Numbers, I was learning, are funny that way.

I had practiced giving injections on an orange. Let me tell you something; your thigh, cellulite aside, is nothing like an orange. For one thing, it feels pain. For another, it's yours. The first night I meticulously laid out my supplies: alcohol wipes, the vials of powdered medication, the sterile water to dilute them, and two syringes, one for each drug. I twisted a long, thick needle onto the first syringe, and, snapping the glass tops off the vials (using gauze to avoid cutting my fingers), I drew up some water, squirted it into the first vial of powder, and gently swirled until it dissolved. Drawing the mixture up, I repeated the process with the next vial and the next. I changed to another needle, about a half inch long, tapping the syringe briskly until all the air bubbles disappeared. I felt very *Medical Center*. Then I pinched some skin with my free hand, took a breath, and jabbed. I couldn't do it. At the last second I pulled my hand back and the needle bounced, barely nicking my flesh. I reminded myself grimly of how much I wanted to have a baby. No, truth: how much I wanted to accomplish pregnancy. I gritted my teeth and jabbed again. Only about fifty more shots to go.

After eleven days a measly four follicles had developed. Doctors like to see at least twice that many, since there's attrition at every stage: not all follicles contain usable eggs, not all eggs will fertilize, and not all fertilized embryos will become babies. Many clinics cancel IVF cycles when there are fewer than five follicles to save the patient additional expense, the heartache of probable failure, and, perhaps, to avoid dinging their own statistics. Dr. Stawecki had another philosophy. "The odds may be low," he told us, "but that's what odds are: they just tell you a likelihood. In my best professional judgment, Peggy, you'll never do any better than this, so what's the point of canceling?"

Steven wasn't convinced. The priciest part of IVF was the egg retrieval surgery. "I thought we agreed not to go ahead if you didn't produce enough eggs," he said. He was right. But I'd already invested so much of my time, energy, and anticipation. I'd already given myself so many shots. Besides, I told Steven, our friend Kristin only produced four follicles and now she and her husband had two-year-old twins. "So you never know," I said.

"That doesn't mean a thing," he countered. "I'm sure there's a supporting anecdote for every situation."

"But if this is as good as it gets . . ."

Exactly thirty-six hours before the egg retrieval was scheduled, Steven injected me with the ovulation-inducing drug. This was a more serious maneuver, using a needle three times as long as the others. It had to go into a specific area on the back of my hip that was difficult for me to reach. I leaned over the bed, my weight on one leg, squeezing my eyes shut.

"Okay," Steven said, "One, two . . ."

I yelped as he hit his mark. "You don't have to do it so hard," I snapped. "It's *skin,* not leather." Then I saw the expression on his face, and realized how much hurting me hurt him.

"Thank you," I said, as he massaged the area to help the medication absorb.

"I'm sorry," he replied.

At 5:30 on a springtime Saturday morning, Steven kissed me good-bye outside the hospital door. He was headed across the street to Dr. Stawecki's office for yet another date with his hand. I was going inside to be prepped for surgery. The procedure had to be timed precisely: if the eggs were harvested too late, I'd ovulate and they'd be lost; too soon, and their outer membranes would be too thick for the sperm to penetrate.

"Good luck," Steven said.

Memory selects; it protects. I recall looking over my shoulder as the hospital door slid shut behind me, seeing Steven still standing there, watching me. I remember the tenderness in his eyes. After that there are only fragments. I see myself lying on a gurney in an operating room, waiting to sink into the oblivion of general anesthesia. I remember Dr. Stawecki telling me he'd harvested only three eggs. I can hear the phone ring twenty-four hours later, the doctor's flat voice telling me only two had fertilized and only one went on to become an embryo.

. "What are my chances now?" I asked.

"Well, they're not zero or we wouldn't move forward," he said, "but after a certain point it doesn't do anyone any good to keep updating the odds."

Four days later, in a cramped room that seemed arbitrarily dark, Steven was once again standing at my head watching someone else between my legs. Dr. Stawecki injected the six-celled ball, tinier than the period at the end of this sentence, into my uterus. I closed my eyes and tried to be pregnant.

"How do you feel?" Steven asked as we left the building.

"Fine," I answered, tartly. "Absolutely fine." I was not going to jinx myself with negative thoughts.

Some doctors put their IVF patients on bed rest for ten days until the pregnancy test; that provides the illusion of doing something productive, though there's no proof that it helps. Dr. Stawecki told me to stay away from the gym and ask the supermarket clerk to bag the groceries extra lightly. I slept more, slacked off on work, and tried my best not to cough. Other than that, Steven and I barely acknowledged what might be happening—dwelling on it would've made those days even harder to bear. After about a week my friend Rachel visited with her two-year-old daughter, one of my favorite children, whom I unthinkingly swept up and spun around in my arms. She weighed nearly thirty pounds. "Oh my God!" I wailed, realizing what I'd done. Rachel tried to comfort me—"If you're pregnant, you're pregnant," she said. "A baby doesn't just fall out of you"—but I was certain I'd blown the one thing over which I actually did have control.

It probably wouldn't have worked anyway.

5

BEST ACTRESS

The Fourth of July was excruciating. You'd think Mother's Day would be the holiday that got me, but although I wasn't a mom myself, I did have one. Independence Day, though, was about family picnics and childhood awe. It evoked memories of sandy potato salad, the itch of mosquito bites, of being sweaty and sticky with ice cream, snuggling on a beach blanket with my brothers to watch fireworks burst across the big Minnesota sky.

July Fourth in the Bay Area was never like that. While the rest of the country sweltered, we guzzled lattes and burrowed deeper into our leather jackets against the summer fog's chill. Still, there were Frisbees and watermelons and children giddy over being allowed to stay up late and play with matches. I couldn't rev myself up for being a good sport, everyone's favorite auntie, so I'd turned down an invitation to a kid-infested barbecue and spent the day in bed. After trying to convince me to go out for a hike, for a movie, for anything,

Steven said he refused to watch me wallow and stalked off to work.

He hadn't come home when the rumbling of the fireworks began, so I'd bundled up and strolled alone to a bare hillside at the end of our street with a view of San Francisco. Way out by the Golden Gate Bridge, I could see the bursts of red and green, made wee and unimpressive by the distance. The sound carried like thunder after lightning, not reaching me until well after the flickering lights faded; their insignificance only made me feel lonelier. Since I'd stopped taking the shots, joy felt as remote to me as those colored sparks. I'd been so leery of being trapped by motherhood, so wary of its threat to my career and marriage, to my hard-won sense of self. Here I was instead, defined by my longing for a child, by my inability to become a mother. Far worse. Far worse.

Our relationship with Dr. Stawecki had fizzled as well. A few days earlier, at a meeting to review our options, his tone had transformed from clinical to curt. I began to see how he'd gotten his mixed reputation. "It was like the difference between the way people talk to you when you've just had a hit movie and when you've made a bomb," Steven said. We had apparently developed the stink of failure.

"You only had one ovary to begin with," the doctor said, "and you had a poor response. Then, of course, you're over thirty-eight years old. So I would say at this point your chances of conceiving with your own eggs are not good." He let that sink in for a moment. "Have you considered using donor eggs?"

"No," I said, stung by the suggestion. "No, we haven't." Just a few weeks earlier he'd held out the promise of IVF. Now suddenly my only shot was to use another woman's eggs? The leap seemed outrageous. Even if he were right, using donor eggs was so *Handmaid's Tale*. Once again I thought, *I'd never be that desperate for a child*.

Dr. Stawecki shrugged. "The other possibility is that you could do injections with insemination every other month and try on your own in between."

"I thought we only had a fifteen-percent chance of conceiving that way," I said. Although cheaper than IVF, drugs and insemination would still cost over three thousand dollars a month.

He nodded. "Yes, but I would say that's your best option."

We said we'd think about it.

"I don't like that he didn't take any responsibility for what happened," Steven grumbled on the way home. "He didn't say anything about the decision to go forward with so few eggs. This doesn't seem like an ideal situation for us to base the next decision on."

Perhaps if the doctor could have owned up to, if not a mistake, at least his own subjectivity, we could have heard the rest of his message more clearly. It was true that I was limited by my age and lone ovary. I hadn't responded well to the drugs. Twelve thousand dollars was a lot to spend on increasingly long odds. Instead it felt like he'd cast the blame on me, that he'd given up on us. I was a strong, accomplished woman, used to being able to make things happen by the force of my steel-toed will. The gauntlet had been thrown down; I wouldn't accept defeat so readily.

"I could call the guy Kristin went to," I said, referring to the friend who'd had twins after producing only four eggs. "Maybe we should consider trying with him."

Steven nodded and put an arm around me. "Don't be blue, P," he said. "I love you more than anything, even my CDs."

I smiled thinly, but I wasn't listening. I was already mentally scanning our calendar, immersed in planning our next try.

"Do you have to be so glum?" Steven said, this time in exasperation. "Can't you think of this as our opportunity to have a baby?"

"No," I sulked. "I can't."

"Then why are we here?"

I looked around unhappily. Our new clinic, in the Pacific Heights neighborhood of San Francisco, was known for treating the posh infertile, though you'd never guess that by the waiting room. The couches were worn, the cushions sagging, and the walls could've done with a coat of paint. The place was packed, mostly with women. Like me, none of them smiled; none acknowledged anyone else's presence. Everyone came in and took a seat as if she were the only person in the room, then stared blank-eyed at her lap or at a back issue of *Town & Country*. I checked them out from the corner of my eye. *What's wrong with the young brunette in the corner?* I wondered. *And that one with the reading glasses—who is she kidding? She has to be at least forty-five!* I knew they were sizing me up, too, guessing at my age, the nature of my defect, which of us had a better shot at success.

Then again, perhaps I was projecting. Maybe, like Steven, everyone else was relieved to be doing something that could result in a child. Maybe they were dreaming of the woman on the clinic's Web site, who gazed adoringly at a gurgling infant, fulfilled. It could be that I was the only one feeling as soiled as the furniture, ashamed that my body didn't work the way it should. Although I'd been the one pushing for this appointment, which took another two months to get, I dreaded the infusion of hope it brought as much as I craved it. "I don't want to have any expectations," I confessed to Steven, as the nurse called our names.

Our new enabler, Daniel Balfour, was the opposite of Dr. Stawecki. Dan, as we called him, was young and good-looking, with none of the older doctor's mystique or paternalism. As earnest and squeaky-clean as a shampoo ad, he was the kind of guy you'd trust to water your lawn and pick up your mail while you were on vacation. He wore a preppie shirt and tie, but no doctor's jacket; his blond hair was boyishly tousled. His online, I'm-human-just-like-you biography said he played the trombone. He was confident that he could do better than Dr. Stawecki. "In my opinion he oversuppressed your natural cycle," Dan said. "That may have made the stimulation harder. I'd try a different protocol and I'd add ICSI after the egg retrieval."

"Icksee?" I said. "What's that?"

"I-C-S-I," he said. "It's an acronym for a relatively new technique that we usually use in male factor infertility. We inject a single sperm into each egg. It will optimize your potential." It was also thought to possibly raise a child's risk of heart defects, chromosomal abnormalities, and, if it were a boy, infertility, though Dan assured us the chances of that were minimal.

"ICSI," I repeated, feeling the rhythm of the word on my tongue. It sounded like one of the Balearic Islands, a party paradise: *Visit the beautiful beaches of Mallorca, Ibiza, and ICSI!* I smiled at Dan. His voice was honeyed, sympathetic, yet seemingly untouched by personal pain. I liked him. I felt we had chemistry, and who knows, maybe that could influence biology. He'd already gotten my friend Kristin pregnant. Plus, my parents, who were as eager as we were for us to conceive, had generously offered to pay for another round of IVF.

"It seems worth a try," I said to Steven. "We can always stop if it doesn't go well"—words I had said before.

"Do you have any tips for success?" I asked as we left.

"Take your prenatal vitamins," the doctor replied. I nodded. Done. "Cut back on coffee and alcohol. There's a small study that says poultry products like eggs and turkey enhance human egg quality. And work on reducing stress." He chuckled. "I wish I had a cure for that one!"

We wouldn't see Dan again for the rest of the cycle. After several examinations by one of his partners, Gary Franklin, I asked a nurse where he was. She seemed surprised. "Dr. Balfour is on vacation," she said.

"But he's why we chose this clinic."

"Oh, all of our doctors are excellent," she replied lightly. Maybe. But it wasn't about competence; I'd picked Dan based on a hunch, on intuition. Now I was in the hands of a man whom I suspected didn't know my name, who probably couldn't pick me out of a line-up unless I were lying on my back naked with my legs spread. I'd never felt so invisible in a doctor's office, so much like parts on an assembly line. But by then I'd been taking the Pill for three weeks to shut down my reproductive system so it could be better manipulated. If I waited until Dan came back, I'd have to stay on it. I couldn't do it—it was too perverse to use birth control for two months in an attempt to get pregnant.

"I have no idea what you're talking about." Steven was lying in bed trying to read while I nattered on about my endometrial lining.

"I've explained this to you a dozen times," I said, impatiently. "The thickness of the lining affects implantation."

"I'm sorry," he said. "I can't remember all the scientific stuff. And frankly I don't really care to."

I bristled. "I go to these appointments every day, the least you can do is try to understand the process."

"I don't mind understanding it, but understanding it and being obsessed with it are two different things."

"Obsessed?" I said. "Let's see you spend all your time poking yourself with needles and getting ultrasound wands shoved inside you and blood drained out of you, and we'll see who's obsessed."

Steven pressed his eyelids with the pads of his fingers. "Can't we please change the subject? Can't we, for just one night, talk about something else?"

"That's easy for you to say. I'm not *doing* anything else," I lashed out at him, but I was angry with myself, with my lemon of an aging body, with fate. Every morning I would drive through rush-hour traffic to the city to be probed, measured, and judged. Then it was out to the 'burbs to a cheapo pharmacy for my drug fix. I could've saved a couple of hours in the car by using my local Walgreen's, but each vial cost twenty dollars more there. I was using eight, a difference of a hundred and sixty dollars a day—nearly two thousand bucks by the time I was through. My first car had cost less than that.

Infertility treatment consumed me, used up all my physical and mental energy. And speaking of consuming . . . I stood up and shoved my feet into my slippers. "If you'll excuse me," I said, stiffly, "I'm going to the kitchen to eat some poultry."

My friend Margaretta, an editor at a women's magazine, called the next morning to offer me a last-minute assignment that would require a trip to Los Angeles. "I can't," I confided. "I'm in the middle of an IVF cycle."

"Oh, God." I could almost feel her recoil from the phone. "I would never want to be back where you are now."

Margaretta had once organized her life around infertility, even staying in a job two years longer than she wanted to, to avoid changing her health insurance. She'd taken Clomid for a year—"That was stupid," she said now—and done one round of IVF. "I had planned to do two more cycles, but I realized we would spend all of our money on IVF, and if it didn't work we wouldn't have enough left over to do anything else. We'd be broke." She and her husband had decided instead to adopt, and ten years ago brought their daughter, Franny, home from Paraguay. Margaretta was one of the happiest moms I knew. She and Franny were about to leave for a mother-daughter vacation in Mt. Zion Park.

I had other acquaintances, five or ten years older than I, who had lost their late thirties down the rabbit hole of infertility, whose lives had been undone by it. I had never considered that the same could happen to me. A few of them eventually delivered miracle babies. Several more, like Margaretta, had adopted. One had divorced, then later remarried and become a stepmother. Each would make a point of telling me that she was content, safely on the other side of the trauma, though she'd shudder to recall the journey. "I wouldn't wish infertility on my worst enemy," another of my editors said. "I don't even like to talk about it." Those exchanges, sometimes just a few minutes long, sustained me. At my worst moments I would replay them in my head, polishing them like lucky charms, like gemstones. They reminded me, even fleetingly, that one way or another this would end, that the way I felt now might not be how I'd feel for the rest of my life.

"There's something I want you to know," Margaretta said, her voice urgent. *"The pain goes away."*

God, I hoped so.

On one of our earliest dates, Steven took me to Los Angeles to attend the Academy Awards. He'd been nominated for a documentary about Estelle Ishigo, a Caucasian artist who'd gone into the internment camps with her Japanese American husband in the 1940s and chronicled the prisoners' lives there. At the ceremony, we were seated near Sinead O'Connor (before the blasphemy charges), Michael Jackson (before the molestation charges), and right next to primatologist Jane Goodall (a competitor in Steven's category, who, apparently having spent too much time with apes, snubbed us).

When actress Phoebe Cates opened the envelope-please and read Steven's name, he didn't move. "You won," I said, feeling like I was speaking through Jell-O, then stood to let him pass. On the tape there is a flash of big hair and aqua sequins before a clip from his film rolls—my nanosecond of fame, witnessed by all of our friends as well as forty-three million strangers. That night imbued our relationship with a fairy-tale glow, a sprinkling of stardust. If part of marriage is developing a mythology of destiny, the Oscar (which now sits on top of our fridge) was integral to ours.

How different things were ten years later, when Steven was nominated for an Emmy, this time for a film he'd made for HBO about young heroin addicts. The awards were scheduled smack in the middle of our IVF cycle, right around the time that whatever embryos we had would be transferred back to my body. I didn't even congratulate him when he told me. "Too bad you can't go" was all I said. Even whacked out on fertility drugs, I should've known that was a mistake. My husband's ancestors are from Mito, a city in Japan whose population is renowned for its stubbornness. I could almost see him dig in his heels.

"I'm not missing it," he said. "And there's no reason you can't go, either."

"You want me to get on a plane right after the embryo transfer?"

"It's not like you'd be running a marathon," he said. "You'd just be hanging out in business class. What's the difference if you sit in a plane or on a couch?"

"You don't know," I said, defensively. "You're not a doctor."

"Then why don't you ask one?"

Dr. Franklin took Steven's side. There was no medical reason for me to stay behind. But my resistance was deeper than that. I wanted to direct all of my energy to pregnancy, to nurse my hopes and delusions in my own bed. More than that, I needed to feel beyond reproach, especially self-reproach.

"Would you be mad if I didn't go?" I asked.

"I'd be disappointed," Steven said. "It's not like we have a lot of fun together anymore." Touché. "But I'm not taking responsibility for the decision. It's your body, it's your choice."

I thought back to the weightlessness I'd felt at the Oscars, the easy love between us in those days. Being together used to be more than enough for me—it was everything. When had that changed? In weighing all the risks of fertility treatments, I had willfully ignored the risks to our relationship.

"Okay," I said, "I'll go. But the doctor said I have to have a wheelchair at the curb at the airport to take me to the gate and one in New York to take me to the taxi. And I'm not leaving the hotel room except to go to the ceremony." I had chosen my marriage over my obsession. Sort of.

Dr. Franklin handed me a black-and-white picture of the three embryos that had grown in the incubator. Magnified to the size of a quarter, each looked like a cluster of soap bubbles surrounded by a fuzzy gray corona. Was I supposed to think of these as my children? Were they anything more than a lab technician's sleight of hand? The doctor pointed to the best of the bunch—four symmetrical cells, each containing the biological flotsam to transform it into a person.

Usually the clinic let embryos develop longer, but we'd

moved the process up in order to catch our flight to New York. "We only recently started waiting the extra time to do the transfer," Dr. Franklin assured us. "It's not clear that it makes a difference."

I handed the photograph to Steven, who stowed it in his wallet. "If this works give that back," I said. "Otherwise I never want to see it again."

I lay on the exam table, and Dr. Franklin slid the embryos inside me. I felt suffused with light. For a single golden moment I knew—I *knew*—I was pregnant. Then the doubts flooded in.

"How do you feel?" Steven asked, just as he had the last time.

"Maybe," I replied.

I spent the next thirty-six hours in the Marriott Hotel in Times Square. Although I'd once lived in this city, I told none of my old friends I was here. A few minutes before the awards, I carefully slipped on a floor-length, hip-skimming burgundy dress and strappy, architecturally high sandals. I dusted my collar bone with glitter and twirled, ever so delicately, in front of Steven.

He beamed. "You look beautiful," he said, as I leaned on his arm like an invalid. "Let's go."

The News and Documentary Emmys are not among those given out on the prime-time show. They were presented at a separate ceremony, by newsmakers and politicians, all male and nearly all white—people like George Pataki, Alan Dershowitz, and a commentator from the *The NewsHour* whom, inexplicably (and erroneously), the evening's host referred to three times as "a handsome guy." PBS, go figure. The statuettes themselves were doled out by sequin-sheathed models—apparently, the

Television Academy's idea of equal opportunity. When Steven's category came up, I played it cool, looking straight ahead while clutching his knee under the table. That night, however, the name they called wasn't his. We smiled and clapped politely as some network producer thanked his third-grade teacher. Later, everyone from HBO—both the winners and the I'm-honored-just-to-be-nominated—retired to the revolving bar on the hotel's top floor. I gazed out the window, sipping sparkling water as the skyline slipped by, detached from the conversation around me. What had I done? I wished I hadn't come; I was glad I did.

Ten days later I would get the results of my blood test. I wasn't pregnant.

"Have you considered donor eggs?" asked Dan at our post-mortem visit. He'd returned from vacation and reclaimed his place as our primary physician. "Our success rates are over sixty percent."

What was with these guys? They dangled IVF in front of us and *after* it failed—and we'd shelled out the cash—said I was a bad candidate for it. What's more, after implying that a genetic link to our baby was so important that it was worth going to physical and financial extremes to attain, they whipped around and implied that the link, at least my link, was no big deal: the key to motherhood was carrying the child, not conceiving it. I wondered whether, if my problem had been a wonky uterus, he'd be insinuating that the vessel didn't matter—anyone could grow a baby—it was the egg that made the mom. It was as if donor eggs were part of a continuum, another "cure" for infertility rather than a huge psychological leap.

I shook my head. Science and me, we were through. "What about trying on our own?" I asked.

"I'd put your chances at about one in three hundred," he replied in that gentle voice of his. Then after a moment: "Of course, there's also adoption."

I felt hollow inside, completely scooped out. I had friends like Margaretta who'd adopted and who, I knew, were eager for me to see the light. But Steven wasn't sure he could handle the potential challenge—"I'm not saying it never works out, but being given up by your mother is a hard thing. I'm not sure I have the strength and wisdom to deal with it"—and I couldn't make the case for it. Adoption still seemed compensatory to me, like a last choice rather than the best one. As long as that was true, as long as I held out the dream of bearing our child myself, I couldn't pursue it.

"We don't recommend any particular agencies," Dan added, "but there are a number of good ones in the city. If you decide that's what you want to do, call and we can get you a list."

That afternoon, leaving the clinic, I felt sprung. No more shots! No more doctors! No more waiting rooms! By now it was October, a full year since I'd started the Clomid. A year of my life gone. I'd hardly noticed the seasons change. The sky as we walked toward the car was gray and stippled. During college, when I'd worked as a lifeguard, I'd learned to read the weather in the clouds; these predicted rain. "Curdled sky, not twenty-four hours dry," I said, half to myself.

Steven looked at me. "What?" he asked.

"Nothing." We walked on silently, not touching. My exuberance began to fade. We weren't having a baby. We might never have a baby. "I blame myself for this," I said, my voice trembling.

Steven sighed. "You have to accept the choices you made, Peg."

I whirled on him. "You weren't supposed to *agree*! You were supposed to hug me and say it would be all right."

"I can't," he said, irritably. "I'm sorry. I can't say something just to make you feel better. That would discount how bad I feel. This *is* partly your fault. You made the decision early on in our marriage not to talk about having children. Okay, it's my fault, too. I could've pushed you harder. But that's the choice I made and I'll have to live with it."

"Are you *trying* to make me feel worse?" I said.

"I'm just saying we have to take responsibility for our actions."

"But if we'd started earlier, I might have found out that I had cancer while I was pregnant. Pregnancy might have made the cancer worse. I might have had to abort. I might have died."

"That's not why we didn't discuss it." I knew he was right, that our situation was a confluence of chance and choice. Admitting that, though, would have overwhelmed me with regret, as if I'd lived my whole life wrong. It was easier to be angry with Steven than to confront my own mistakes.

"I can't believe this," I said. I leaned against an apartment building, watched a woman roll by with a double-wide stroller. "I don't know what to do."

Steven's voice softened a little, whether out of affection or exhaustion I wasn't sure. "I don't think we should do anything right now. I think we should wait awhile and then discuss it.

And although I don't like what it's doing to us, I guess we should go back to having fertility sex. I don't care what Dan said—that's the only thing so far that's worked."

"Really?" I said. "You'd do that?"

"Yes, but P, you have to care about something else besides getting pregnant. We have to have a life as well."

"Okay," I said, sniffling a little. "I will."

He looked at me sharply.

"Seriously," I insisted, crossing my heart. "I promise."

6

SHIKATAGANAI

Perched on the back of a mint green Vespa, I serpentined through Roppongi, Tokyo's Westerners' ghetto as well as its nightly wet dream for sexually deprived white males with an Asian fetish. Miniskirted Japanese lovelies trawl clubs with names like Gas Panic for Caucasian boyfriends. Filipinas with a yen for yen cozy up to guys who could never land a date back home.

I had met the man whose waist I clung to—a tall, shaven-headed American—about thirty seconds earlier. He was a friend of a friend, a fellow journalist who'd phoned me for a drink within moments of my arrival from the airport. When he pulled up in front of International House, a residence for visiting scholars where I was spending the next two months, with an extra helmet in tow, I thought, *Why not?* and hopped on.

I was in Tokyo on a grant, reporting a story on young Japanese women who were rejecting marriage and motherhood.

Well into their thirties, they lived at home with their parents, paying no rent, coming and going as they pleased while Mom cooked their meals and did the laundry. With no living expenses, they splurged on Louis Vuitton, Bulgari, Fendi, Prada. Their spending sprees were keeping the economy afloat, but their refusal to buckle down and make babies was causing a crisis. Japan's birthrate was among the lowest in the world; soon there wouldn't be enough young workers to support the pensions and health care costs of the rapidly aging population. Everyone—politicians, economists, the media—blamed these women, whom they bluntly referred to as "parasite singles."

I had been to Japan before, but always with Steven, who sometimes worked with Japanese TV. Although he doesn't speak the language, he knows his Tokyo. I'd never so much as gone for a walk by myself. Nor did I want to; few of the city's narrow, twisting streets have names, and the addresses are based on when a building was built rather than where it's located. So number 3 could be next door to number 165. Locals rarely refer to addresses anyway. When scheduling an interview, they'd faxed me a map and directions based on landmarks: take the number 4 exit from the subway, look for the police kiosk and turn right, walk until you see a 7-Eleven and turn left. It was just as well; since I was illiterate in Japanese, I wouldn't have been able to read street signs.

Steven was supposed to be with me on this trip, too, but he had just started a new film and couldn't get away. He told me to go anyway, to have an adventure on my own. It would be the first time in nine years we'd been separated for more than a few days, but a break didn't seem like a bad idea. We'd been back at "fertility sex" for four months, and whenever the time drew near we would begin to argue. Not just to argue, but to flay one another raw. He accused me of breaking my promise, of treating him like a sperm bank with legs. He threatened to go on strike. "You're not having a relationship if this is all you care about, Peg," he said. "I want to have a baby, too, but I want to have a life more."

That made me frantic; I needed him, or at least needed his semen. I would swear again to stop being obsessive, even offer, theoretically, to skip a month of trying. I'd tell him he was right about whatever had sparked that month's battle, anything, anything to convince him to come to bed. Rather than mocking Babyfever, I now sympathized with her. Hell, I had *become* her.

I planned my trip both to ensure we would be together when I ovulated and to keep Steven from realizing I was doing so. My flight to Tokyo took off about a week after February's try. Claiming I would miss him terribly, I proposed a rendezvous in Hawaii (about halfway between us) three weeks later. I then suggested he join me in Tokyo about a month after that, when my reporting would be largely done, so we could salvage a week or so of sightseeing before I came home. Even I knew I was being pathological. It was insanity to meet in Hawaii. I didn't even want to. It would jeopardize my research and his production schedule. But what if that was the only month for the rest of my life that I would be able to get pregnant? What if this was the only way we could have a baby? That was ludicrous, I'd tell myself. Wasn't it?

Inflicting your Western Otherness on Japan's homogeneity can feel like an act of violence. The culture pushes back, resists the assault, reminds you that you are firmly and forever an out-sider. Not American or European or Canadian, but a generic, all-purpose *gaijin*—a foreigner—free of expectations, divorced from consequence, treated like a capricious child. In that state, time can feel suspended along with the roles and rules of life back home. It's liberating in a way, perhaps too much so. I was relieved to escape my embattled marriage, to avoid the stand-offs over what to do next. Being in Tokyo was like being twenty-five again without the worries, now so quaint, over a fledgling career or a noncommittal boyfriend.

Which brings me back to the man on the Vespa. We zipped under the elevated freeway and sped past Almond, the frothy pink bakery that is Roppongi's central meeting spot. I pressed my cheek against his back to avoid the biting wind and thought, *Is this me? Is this me riding on an Italian scooter with a man I don't know when my husband is five thousand miles away? Is this me alone in a strange city, in a strange country where I can't speak the language? Is this really me?*

I didn't have to mention to this man that I was married. I could have played out the fantasy, convinced myself that it didn't really count since I was so far from home. How easy it would have been to start over, how sweet to be free, just for an evening, of the baggage of my relationship. Although I would soon prove myself capable of any number of self-deceptions, however, be-ing *Lost in Translation* wasn't one of them. Despite our troubles, I loved Steven, and I brought his name into the evening's con-versation with almost Tourette-like frequency. Whether it was that or some other disconnect, the tryst sputtered within twenty minutes. The man didn't object when I offered to walk back alone.

My room at "I-House" was modest, dormlike: a lumpy single bed, a beat-up desk, a chair, a TV, and a sink with a mirror. Toilets and showers were down the hall. A sliding glass door led to a small balcony overlooking a snowy Japanese garden. A sign in the hallway warned against leaving "personal items" outside because "the crows might make mischief with them." Ignoring that fractured advice, I stowed a three-pound bag of tangerines in the corner nearest the door. An hour later, I saw it sail across the garden clutched in a black bird's claws.

My routine during those first days was ascetic, sometimes lonely. After my interviews, which because I needed an interpreter took twice as long as usual, I would return to my room with take-out sushi and watch the English-language movie channel on TV. For two weeks *Rocky* played nightly. I had the Burgess Meredith part down cold. ("Like the guy says, you're gonna eat lightning and you're gonna crap thunder.") Sometimes I would wander down the hall to visit my new colleague, Doug, another homesick journalist. I didn't have much energy for anything else. I couldn't seem to shake my jet lag. I remained perpetually, deep-in-my-bones tired. Suspiciously so.

Sometime, just for a laugh, try buying a pregnancy test in a country where you don't speak the language. I pretended to rock a baby and was offered diapers. I pantomimed a swollen stomach and was given antacid. I considered making a cruder gesture, but figured that would probably get me a pack of condoms. Finally, the pharmacist rustled up an English speaker; by then I was so humiliated that I slunk out of the store without asking her to translate the test's instructions. No matter—two pink lines are two pink lines in any language. I didn't even really need to go through the ritual—I knew the signs; I was five weeks pregnant.

I was also jubilant. I'd done it. I had beaten the odds. I danced a victory jig on top of my bed, holding the plastic stick aloft. "Screw those infertility jerks," I crowed. "They know nothing."

I tucked away the test as a souvenir for the baby (whom, I was sure, would be thrilled to have Mom's old, dried-up pee) and called Steven across the Pacific.

"Are you sure?" he asked, incredulous.

"Of course I am. Do you think I should come home?"

"It's up to you. I'm sure there are English-speaking doctors there."

I considered: I'd rather be under Risa's care, but that would mean more flying during the first trimester, and I wasn't convinced that was safe. I wanted to be with Steven, but not back in the crossfire of our marriage.

"I suppose people have babies here all the time," I finally said. "I guess I'll stay."

He said he would cancel the Hawaii trip (my pretense of romance hadn't fooled him) and buy a ticket to Tokyo instead. He could be there by the pregnancy's ninth week.

Then he changed the subject. Or at least that's how I remember it. Steven recalls telling me repeatedly to stay on an even keel, not to dwell on either best or worst case scenarios. That could well be right. Maybe it was distance and isolation, an insatiable need for reassurance, or simply his refusal to indulge my ping-ponging moods that made it seem like he expressed neither enthusiasm nor much interest, that, over subsequent weeks he barely mentioned the pregnancy again. Either way I know this much is true: I couldn't forget it for a minute.

Instead of him, I confided in Doug, who listened as well as he could from the foreign land of a twenty-five-year-old male. He brought me a pot of spring buttercups to celebrate—something that grew and bloomed. When I told him about the power of poultry products, he dropped off meals of teriyaki chicken and sweet omelet sushi, just in case they'd help even after conception. After a while the I-House staff began to gossip about us, even transferred one of Steven's 7 A.M. calls to Doug's room when I didn't answer my phone. (I was in the shower at the time.) They weren't entirely wrong. Although our relationship was beyond reproach, at that time Doug felt like the closest thing to a husband I had.

Finding an English-speaking obstetrician wasn't difficult, especially in Roppongi. Dr. Sayoko Makabe was just a ten-minute walk from I-House. An assortment of affluent, pregnant *gaijin*—Danes, Australians, Egyptians—filled the chairs that lined the waiting room and continued halfway down the hall. After a two-hour wait I was shown to an examination room. I stripped and sat on what looked like a pink dentist's chair tricked out with metal stirrups. Dr. Makabe came in, said a brisk hello, and pressed a series of hydraulic buttons that lifted and tilted it slightly back. I was essentially still upright and feeling considerably less vulnerable than on a Western-style table. Dr. Makabe's English was reasonably good—she'd completed her training on an American military base—but that didn't necessarily make communication easier. She popped a vaginal ultrasound wand inside me without warning, without so much as an "Excuse me, but now I'm going to shove a giant, penis-shaped hunk of plastic inside your body."

"I think I'm about six weeks along," I said, wincing. "Is everything okay?"

"Too early to tell," she said. "But yes, don't worry, it is fine."

She lowered the chair and scribbled out a prescription for Chinese herbs, explaining that Japanese doctors are schooled in both Eastern and Western techniques.

"To prevent miscarriage," she said, handing it to me. "Fill it at the pharmacy downstairs."

I hesitated. "Don't worry," she continued. "It won't hurt the baby. Dissolve it in boiling water and drink. Like tea."

I didn't bother explaining that I had no access in my room to boiling water. I tried mixing the herbs in the hottest water from my sink's tap, but they lay like sludge at the bottom of the cup. In the end, I took a swig of tepid water, poured the herbs in my mouth, and swished. I would spend the next several hours picking grit from my teeth.

Over the following weeks I monitored every twinge. Was that a cramp? Oh, God! A flicker of nausea? Thank goodness! In the midst of interviewing a woman on the advantages of childlessness, I sprinted to the bathroom to vomit. It was humiliating (not to mention ironic), but at least I knew I was still pregnant. I amassed a new set of talismans: a tiny, mottled Buddha that I found at a flea market; a fertility charm I'd bought at the Meiji Shrine; a postcard of a female deity whose name I didn't know. I set them on the shelf above the sink and appealed to them each morning and evening as I brushed my teeth. That, I figured, couldn't hurt the baby, either.

The Japanese women I interviewed seemed to have no interest in having kids. "Once you become a mother, you're *only* a mother," explained Ami, a thirty-three-year-old secretary with fashionably lightened chestnut hair and a Chanel bag. "You're not a woman anymore. You can't work anymore. And the father's not involved. It's very confining. It limits your activities, your financial freedom." She wrinkled her nose in distaste and added, "It's really not attractive." Her mother would probably agree; in one recent survey, the majority of Japanese women over fifty had said they found marriage disappointing and motherhood a burden. What's more, they'd told that to their adult daughters, encouraging them to stay single. At the same time, the younger women weren't interested in becoming the woman in the gray flannel kimono, either, slaving round-the-clock at their offices the way Japanese men do. They weren't sure what they wanted. "I'm thinking maybe I'll try mountain climbing some day," Ami said dreamily. "Maybe I'd be passionate about that."

After a while I noticed the odd-sounding word *wagamama* coming up in nearly every interview. When I asked about it, my interpreter, an aspiring film producer who was herself a "parasite," laughed. "It doesn't translate exactly," she said. The closest she could come was "selfish" or "willful," but in a culture where personal sacrifice is the highest virtue, the connotation was far harsher, especially for women. The parasites had taken on the word as a term of defiance—somewhat like the way American women use "girl" or African Americans say "nigga"—transforming its meaning to something closer to "choosy" or even "self-determining." Women's magazines had caught the trend, featuring headlines like "Restaurants for the Wagamama You." One afternoon I even walked by an office building on which WAGAMAMA was painted in English letters ten stories high. I began asking my subjects if they were *wagamama*. They would initially startle, but then, with some self-mockery, accept the label. It had clearly become a kind of resistance against narrow expectations.

Inevitably, they would also point to Crown Princess Masako as the justification for their behavior. Her life story served as a warning, a kind of reverse fairy tale. Before her marriage, Masako Owada had graduated magna cum laude from Harvard, spoke five languages, lived in four countries, and pursued a glamorous career as a diplomat. Prince Naruhito proposed three times before she succumbed, many believe out of a sense of duty to family and country. Young women all over Japan held their breath: a woman so vibrant, so unapologetically modern, would surely drag the monarchy into the twenty-first century— or at the very least out of the tenth—and the rest of Japan along with it. Instead, from the moment Masako donned her Shinto wedding costume—a wax-encrusted wig and thirty-pound, twelve-layer kimono—she began to fade away, receding under the weight of tradition until she was nearly invisible. She walked several paces behind her husband, eyes downcast, a forced smile on her face. She abandoned foreign travel. She spoke so infrequently that during a rare press conference in 1997, her vocal cords gave out after just three questions. Most important, her worth as a person became contingent on bearing a male heir to the Chrysanthemum Throne. So far, in seven years of marriage, she'd had only one pregnancy, which had ended in miscarriage. After that she retreated even further from the public eye. (Shortly after I left Japan, the Imperial Household Agency announced that the princess was again pregnant. The baby, however, turned out to be a girl so can't rule unless succession laws are changed. Masako soon stopped appearing in public entirely. In 2004 it was revealed that she was undergoing treatment for depression.)

I was tempted to pity Masako—and all Japanese women—to feel smug in my American opportunities and choices. Yet how many of my friends had made professional compromises that they'd never ask of their husbands? How many had abandoned personal dreams and wrapped themselves in the mantle of traditional motherhood? How *wagamama* were we willing to be? Hadn't that been one of my greatest concerns about motherhood? And what about me? How was it that despite my achievements, my education, my professed feminist politics, my self-worth had been reduced to whether or not I could produce a child? As I choked down my herbs, I often thought of

Masako; the silenced princess may be a bigger part of our own psyches than we'd care to admit.

I wasn't lonely anymore. I felt a current, almost like a silvery thread, running between me and my little zygote. Once again I named him Kai—I was certain that this one, too, was a boy. I imagined his little bundle of cells burrowing safely into my belly, settling in for the nine-month ride. I talked to him while I showered, sang to him before falling asleep. Each morning, I would describe our walk to the subway, pulling my thin jacket tight around us against the bitter winds of March. (A Californian by predilection if not by birth, I was chronically underdressed for the season.) One day, when I was nearly eight weeks pregnant, I noticed that the trendy clothing shop on our corner had transformed overnight into an even trendier café. That was Japan, I joked to Kai. Perhaps tomorrow it would be an Italian restaurant.

Suddenly I felt the thread, that silvery strand connecting us, snap. Just like that. "It's over," I whispered and started to cry.

At my next appointment Dr. Makabe again jabbed her ultrasound wand inside me. She poked around and frowned.

"No heartbeat," she said.

I squeezed my eyes shut trying to push down the dread. "What's wrong?" I asked.

She shrugged. "The egg sac is a little large and that can sometimes . . . well, not sometimes, but *rarely* indicate a chromosome abnormality."

"What are the chances that's the case?"

She frowned again. "Percentage? I'd say eighty percent that

everything is okay. It's still early to see a heartbeat. I will see you next week."

The first magazine feature I ever wrote was a posthumous profile of Atsuko Chiba, a Japanese journalist who penned a newspaper column in the early 1980s about her struggle with, and ultimate death from, breast cancer. This was before I had the disease myself, before I'd visited—or ever thought of visiting—Japan. It was uncanny how the themes of her life had resurfaced in my own. One of the things Chiba wrote was that Japanese doctors lie to protect their patients' feelings. It's considered legitimate, for instance, to withhold a cancer diagnosis from a woman even after a mastectomy so that she won't fall into a suicidal funk. So I didn't believe Dr. Makabe.

I e-mailed Risa; she wrote back that the heartbeat should indeed be visible by now. "It doesn't look good," she said. "But she's right to wait another week to be sure."

"How do you feel?" Steven asked when I called to tell him.

"Numb," I said. "Sad." Sadder than sad. My heart constricted around my sorrow, held it close, rocked it like . . . a child.

"Me too," he said. Again, I considered going home, but although it wasn't as bad as the first time, I was still so sick. I hated throwing up on planes. Besides, Japan has one of the highest abortion rates in the world. The Pill was virtually illegal there until recently, so condoms, and as a result abortions, are the primary methods of birth control. I wouldn't let a local dentist fill a cavity, but a D&C? That's one medical procedure the Japanese ought to do well. Once more I opted to stay.

I spent the next seven days, an eternity, enough time to create a world, trying to argue myself out of my certainty. What if my negativism caused a miscarriage, if my doubts made my fears come true? My friend Eva back home tried to rein me in. "If you could think your way to a miscarriage, there would be no unwanted babies," she wrote in an e-mail. "There would be no teenage mothers." I threw away my talismans in case they were having the opposite of their intended effect, in case they were somehow cursed. I mentally scanned my body to see if I could rekindle that tiny filament. I couldn't. I knew I wouldn't.

"The egg sac is empty," Dr. Makabe intoned when she looked at the wavy lines of the ultrasound screen. She lowered my pink padded chair. "*Shikataganai*," she added. It can't be helped.

"Do you want to go or not?" Steven said, barely controlling his impatience.

"I don't know," I stammered. "Yes. I mean no. I mean, I want to want to but . . ."

Whatever psychic glue held me together over the previous weeks dissolved when I picked up Steven at Narita Airport. It was not what he'd expected. He was disappointed, too, but the pregnancy had been more abstract to him. I had discovered it thousands of miles from home. When I miscarried, I was still an ocean away. Nothing had changed for him, nothing tangible had happened. So he was unprepared, perhaps naively so, for the force of my misery, for the sheer wretchedness of the woman who fell sobbing into his arms.

Weeks before, when I still believed I was pregnant, we had discussed spending a couple of nights of his visit in Hakone, a popular resort area outside Tokyo. Now I didn't want to go. Until the D&C, which was scheduled in five days, I would still feel the seasickness and exhaustion of pregnancy, sensations all the more unpleasant since there'd be no reward for them. At the same time, I didn't want to disappoint Steven—he'd come all this way, how could I say I just wanted to lie in bed and watch *Rocky*?

"I don't care what we do," he said. "I'm not asking you to be a martyr by saying you want to do things that are 'fun' and then complaining the whole time that you don't feel well. I'll stay within your limits if you tell me what they are. Just don't expect me to read your mind."

I should've said, "Honey, I feel lousy. I can't eat. I'm nauseous and depressed. I know you wanted to have fun, but I'm not capable of it." Yet, I couldn't. I felt too guilty about feeling sick, too guilty about losing another pregnancy. I wanted to do what would make him happy, but I was too far gone to know what that might be. Instead, I did just the opposite.

"Okay," I said, lifting my voice a notch above leaden. "Let's go."

There are few undiscovered vacation spots in Japan. Mostly, the only places to go are those where everyone goes. The only ways to explore are the ways everyone explores. The Way to See Hakone is to ride through on its various fanciful forms of transport. After getting off the train from Tokyo, we boarded a tram that cut switchbacks up a mountainside into the town of Gora, where the hotel was. From there we took a cable car ride to an art museum (which was closed until summer). Next, onto a ropeway that swayed precariously above a vast, volcanic crater whose fumaroles billowed yellow steam. A pirate's ship worthy of a Disney set ferried us on the last leg of our journey, across four-hundred-thousand-year-old Lake Ashi, with its waters that mirrored a view of Mt. Fuji. Then finally we took a bus back to the hotel.

How could I have brought us on a trip involving so many things that rocked, swung, lurched, or heaved? I was miserable; Steven was sullen. "Why are we here?" he asked as we crossed the crater.

"I thought it was what you wanted."

"Jeez, Peg, sometimes you're so eager to please that you don't even listen to what I'm saying." We looked out opposite windows and I held my breath against the crater's sulfurous reek.

Charlie Chaplin had been a guest at the Fuji-ya Hotel, where we were staying. So had Franklin Roosevelt, Clark Gable, Albert Einstein, and John and Yoko. But these days it looked like something from *The Shining*. The carpets in the underlit hallways were stained. The mattress in our room sagged. The floor sagged, too. The bathroom taps, which ran water from natural hot springs, took fifteen minutes to warm up. Even the bellhops looked dusty. There was an inviting mosaic-tiled indoor pool, but we hadn't brought suits. So we ate French food served by diffident waiters at the hotel's restaurant (where they forced Steven to put on an antediluvian, and mismatched, tie and jacket) then retired to our room to play Scrabble. That was better. As long as neither I nor the surface I was sitting on moved, I was okay; I could even enjoy myself. The serrated edge in our voices began to smooth. We laughed about the kitschy pirate ship and the overcooked lamb shanks. We started to feel like "us" again, at last.

That night as we drifted off to sleep, I whispered to Steven, "I'm so sad. And I'm scared."

He shrugged. "You have to learn to roll with it, Peg."

I sat up. "Roll with it?" I repeated.

"You have to be semi-objective."

"Semi-objective?" I exploded. "*Screw you!* I've been alone and puking in a foreign country for a month. For the last week I've known I wasn't pregnant and had to feel like crap anyway. In two days I'm getting my insides scraped out." Finally, an excuse to let go, to rant, to wail. I would've spewed sulfur myself if I could have. "Why should I be objective? I'm angry and upset, and I hate myself for not having babies when I was thirty, because now I'm obviously going to run out of time."

"I know you want me to be sympathetic, but I'm not," Steven shot back. "I've run out of sympathy. I'm tired of your self-absorption. I'm tired of how you make this all about you. I'm tired of how in love you are with your own misery. You are not the only one in pain here."

That stung. So maybe I had cast him as a bit player in my own personal opera. Maybe I had considered his feelings beside the point (if I'd considered them at all). But at that moment I didn't care. My rage—at fate, at him, at myself—would brook no remorse. "Maybe," I sneered, "you just have to *roll with it.*" I lay back down, seething, glaring at the ceiling. Steven didn't apologize. Neither did I.

D&Cs are a two-day affair in Japan. On the first morning, Dr. Makabe inserted four match-sized sticks of compressed seaweed, called laminaria, into my cervix. Over twenty-four hours, each stick was supposed to swell to the size of a pencil in a slow, steady dilation. That sounded fine to me. Natural.

"Will it hurt?" I asked.

"No," she replied. "Maybe a little."

I forgot my own caveat about Japanese doctors. I believed her.

We'd checked into the Tokyo Hilton for the rest of Steven's stay. (A bathroom of our own! What luxury!) By the time we got there, an hour later, I was doubled over in pain. The cramps came in long, slow-breaking waves. My cervix was indeed dilating—I was in labor. I called the clinic and demanded to speak with Dr. Makabe.

"I am in extreme pain," I gasped as another cramp washed over me.

"Can you *gaman*?" she said. *Gaman* is a fundamental Japanese precept. It means persevering at all costs, suffering in silence. As it happens, I'm not Japanese.

"No!" I said. "I cannot *gaman*. I can't even stand."

She suggested I take some ibuprofen. "*Gambatte*," she said and hung up. Also key to the Japanese character, *gambatte* means "Do your best. Don't quit." In this case I suspect it was closer to "Suck it up, loser."

I lay curled in a ball on the bathroom floor, hoping the cold tiles would distract me from my pain. Steven flipped around the TV channels with the remote, saying little. In general, our cultural differences add zing to our marriage, a welcome shake of spice. On the issue of complaint, however, that spice is red-hot chili pepper. I'm a Jew—I consider kvetching my birthright, a way to connect to those I love, to communicate. If I have a hangnail, you're going to hear about it. Like many people of Japanese descent—particularly from the samurai class that his great-great-grandmother was part of—Steven calls complaining *monku*-ing and to him it's shameful, the worst thing you can do. He is the most compassionate person I know except when his *monku* radar gets tripped—even if the self-pity that sets it off is justified.

"You could've asked a Japanese friend to go over the procedure with you," he said calmly. "They would have warned you; I would've brought over some Vicodin. You didn't even try to prepare."

I was as close to hating him as I had ever been. So what if he was right? Why rub my face in it when I'm lying prostrate beneath a hotel room sink? I just wanted chicken soup and sympathy.

The cramps subsided later that night, and I slept for a few hours before heading back to Dr. Makabe's office, where she would perform the procedure. Although seemingly unconcerned with the discomfort caused by the expanding seaweed sticks, she used general anesthetic for a D&C. I lay down on a table with stirrups that were set much too short for my five-foot, eight-inch frame. My legs jutted out into the center of the room. The nurses kept whacking into them and giggling. "*Sumimasen*," they would repeat each time with a slight bow—excuse me.

Dr. Makabe came in to administer the anesthesia. "This will put me to sleep, right?" I asked anxiously.

She cocked her head, considering, her syringe poised in the air. "It puts Japanese women to sleep," she mused. "I don't know about foreigners."

Get me the hell out of here was my last thought before everything went black.

The next morning it snowed—almost unheard of in Tokyo in late March. The powder settled onto the pink and fuchsia blooms of the plum trees, drifted onto the cherry trees, which were just beginning to loosen the grip on their buds. I already felt like myself again. Steven and I lay in bed wiling away the day with a haiku contest, taking turns writing verse about the weather, the straight-backed old ladies on their black bicycles, about love. I felt like one of the bruised but unbowed characters of a Yasujiro Ozu film.

"Let's just say good-bye here," Steven said when it was time for him to go. He didn't even want me to walk him to the subway station. I nodded, didn't cry. Our love had become so caught in recriminations, so buried in layers of misunderstanding. He drew me to him. "It's over," he said. He was referring to the miscarriage, the surgery. At least I hoped he was.

7

CHERRY BLOSSOM HEARTS

The Shinkansen, Japan's bullet trains, travel at speeds of 187 miles per hour, the fastest land transport in the world. They connect virtually every major city in the country. They are never late. They are never early. You can set your watch by their schedule, and you'd better or you'll be in danger of missing them. Three days after Steven left, at precisely 10:04 A.M., I boarded a Nozomi bullet train to Hiroshima. I'd planned the trip weeks before, and as when I'd zipped off to St. Louis after my previous miscarriage, there seemed no reason to cancel. I would only mope in Tokyo; better, I thought, to bury myself in work.

Steven's first film had been about atomic bomb survivors, or *hibakusha* as they're called in Japanese; through him I had developed my own passion for the subject, and was considering writing a novel about the fate of women and children in the years after the Bomb was dropped. No one, neither Japanese nor American, likes to dwell on the discrimination survivors faced from the outsiders who poured into the city after the war, the presumption that their radiation-induced wounds were contagious. Young women in particular, visibly scarred or not, became pariahs, shunned for fear they'd bear deformed children.

On previous visits I'd befriended several "Hiroshima Maidens": twenty-five young women whom *Saturday Evening Post* editor Norman Cousins, along with a group of Quaker families, brought to New York in 1955 for reconstructive surgery. They were our country's first glimpse of the Bomb's victims. Photographs of Hiroshima were still classified at that time, and President Truman told the press that the Bomb exploded over a military target. Even if he'd told the truth, Americans, who had been subject to years of anti-Japanese propaganda and still mourning their own dead sons, weren't inclined to be sympathetic. But the Maidens' plight transcended all of that. One woman's face was reduced to pulp, her lips and nose seared off, her chin fused to her neck. Another had webs of red, ropy keloids stretching from her face to her wrists. A third had no eyelids. Cousins chose shrewdly; the Maidens, who had been junior high and high school students in 1945, were embraced as innocent victims, broken creatures whom America, in its postwar largesse, would fix both physically and spiritually.

"The girls," as they were known, became a media sensation, appearing on the cover of *Life*, shown in *Collier's* eating hotdogs at Yankee Stadium, and publishing bubbly "diary entries" in women's magazines. The man who accompanied them, Methodist minister Kiyoshi Tanimoto—a protagonist of John

Hersey's *Hiroshima*—was celebrated on *This Is Your Life* (though the Maidens who appeared with him were veiled by a screen to avoid upsetting viewers). He would go on to become the world's most famous *hibakusha*, criss-crossing America giving lectures and raising money, even offering an opening prayer on the floor of the U.S. Senate.

The Reverend Tanimoto had died in the 1980s, but I wrote to his wife, Chisa, who still lived in Hiroshima, requesting an interview about their years with the Maidens. She replied that she'd be pleased to meet me, but first I'd have to be screened by her oldest daughter, Koko, a minister's wife herself who lived in Osaka. That was easy enough—I could stop there on my way down to Hiroshima.

My interpreter in Tokyo had told me to grab a cab at Osaka Station and tell the driver to take me to Kita-Senri Church, which was a short ride away. She neglected, however, to tell me the Japanese word for church. "Kita-Senri" is the name of the neighborhood; it would be like repeating "Upper West Side" over and over to a New York cabbie and expecting him to take you to St. John the Divine. Still, Christian churches are unusual in Japan. How hard could it be to figure it out? I fumbled for a pen, drew a house with a cross on top, and showed it to the driver.

A travel tip: Japanese will never say they can't help you. If a clerk doesn't have your size at a department store, she'll hem and haw and bring you random merchandise until you go away. Although he nodded vigorously, my cab driver had no idea where I wanted to go. He drove around Osaka, stopping occasionally and opening the automatic door, hoping I would take the hint and get out. On his third attempt to dump me, in front of a nondescript apartment building, he left the meter running and refused to close the door. I wasn't about to get out of a cab in the middle of nowhere in a strange city. So I tried again. I clasped my hands in prayer and looked reverently upward. Nothing. I repeated "Jesus" several times. No luck. Then I sang "Silent Night," followed by "Jesus Christ Superstar." His face lit up. "Ah!" he said. "Christo!" and, to our mutual relief, quickly drove to my destination.

Koko Tanimoto Kondo was waiting for me outside, craning her neck to look down the street, impatiently bouncing on the balls of her feet. A round woman in her mid-fifties, she was surprisingly plainspoken for a Japanese and remarkably short; when we stood side by side, her eyes were level with my ribs. Neither her parents nor her siblings were so tiny, she explained, leading me into the church. She suspected her growth was stunted by radiation exposure. Koko was one of the youngest *hibakusha*, an eight-month-old in her mother's arms when their house collapsed. Mrs. Tanimoto was knocked unconscious and might have remained where she was, dazed, if it weren't for Koko's cries. Instead, she instinctively dug both herself and the baby out of the rubble and fled. Their house burned, but mother and daughter lived.

Like many children of great men, Koko spoke cautiously about her father, but admitted she was jealous of his relationships with the Maidens. "Everyone was so interested in them," she recalled. "He didn't pay much attention to me. I felt left out, like I wasn't important."

Koko grew up defined by the Bomb, always in the shadow of her family name. She hated it. Later, as a college student in Washington, D.C., she claimed to be from Tokyo. She confided the truth only once, in her twenties, to her Chinese American fiancé. He immediately called off the engagement. "I was so angry," she said. "I thought, 'If there is a God, why did he let this happen to me?' I didn't want anything to do with that kind of God."

Koko eventually returned to Japan, settling in Tokyo and marrying an atheist documentary filmmaker named Yasuo Kondo. But film is a fickle business; short on money, the couple was forced to move back to Hiroshima, where Yasuo took a job with his father-in-law at the Peace Center. The two men took long walks in the evening, debating the existence of God. Apparently, the minister won—a few years later, over Koko's objections, Yasuo entered the seminary. "So I've come full circle," she said. "Me! A minister's wife working for peace." She shrugged, a Buddhist to her Christian core. "I guess this is my *en*, my destiny."

The Reverend Tanimoto bequeathed his daughter something else: a commitment to finding homes for orphans. Adoption is rare in Japan, where blood ties determine everything from marriage prospects to career potential. It would be difficult for a Japanese to view someone else's child as her own. What's more, the country's Buddhist culture considers a person born to his *en*. If you are orphaned, well, *shikataganai*. You must *gaman*.

As a Christian, Reverend Tanimoto thought differently. Thousands of elementary school students had been evacuated from Hiroshima to the countryside the spring before the bombing to protect them from possible air raids. They returned to find their parents vaporized, their homes incinerated. In a city of tragedies, there was nowhere for them to go. Some were taken in by extended family. Others were rounded up and shipped to Dickensian orphanages. The rest huddled near the railroad station, begging and stealing to survive. Many of the girls were coerced into prostitution; the boys into becoming "human bullets" in *yakuza* gang wars. It is another part of the past that goes unmentioned. Reverend Tanimoto placed as many children abroad as he could, running what was essentially an adoption agency out of his home. Long after the Bomb orphans had grown, young women continued leaving newborns at his door, desperate to spare both the child and themselves the taint of illegitimacy.

Koko herself was unable to bear children. She believes that this, too, was a result of radiation exposure, though no one can say for sure. In the church office she introduced me to one of her two adopted daughters, a gangly teenager, who looked up from her homework, pushed up her glasses, and smiled shyly. "*Harro*," she said in charmingly accented English. "Pleased to meet you."

That was all it took. Rather than interviewing Koko, I confided in her, spilled the details of my pregnancies and miscarriages. "Just last week?" she said, touching my hand. I nodded, struggling not to cry. "There is a doctor in Hiroshima," she continued. "Occasionally, because of my father's work, she asks me to find a home in America for a baby. It's not predictable— sometimes I get three babies in three months, sometimes I don't get one for two years." She went on to say that the birth mothers were usually teenagers who didn't realize they were pregnant and didn't get abortions in time. Or the babies were products of extramarital affairs. I felt adrenalin course through me. "And once in a while," she said, eyeing me carefully, "they are the babies of rape victims."

I nodded. "It's not the children's fault," I said, with more conviction than I felt. Could I really adopt the child of a rapist? What surprises would lurk in those genes? My outward response, however, was the one Koko was looking for. She smiled. I had passed her test. What's more, she was familiar with Steven's work. We even had a mutual friend in California, Berkeley Symphony conductor Kent Nagano. If he vouched for us, she said, she would put us at the top of her adoption list. I assured her we were interested, though again, I didn't know if that was true.

Koko hugged me as I left, promising to call her mother on my behalf. "She is caring for a baby boy right now who is being adopted by an American," she said. "You can see him, too."

I boarded the train to Hiroshima feeling energized. Maybe this was fate. Maybe all of my work in Hiroshima, all of Steven's work, was destined to lead us here, to Koko, to an adopted Japanese child. On the few occasions when we had discussed adoption, ethnicity had been a sticking point. Adopting a white baby, even if we could find one, seemed wrong for Steven. I suggested a Chinese or Korean child, but he rejected that, too, given Japan's atrocities against those countries during World War II. "That would be like a German adopting an Israeli," he said. I nixed Latin America, reluctant to raise someone from a staunchly Catholic culture as a Jew. We never imagined we'd be

115

able to find a baby in Japan. I began drafting a letter to Koko confirming our interest and asking for more details. Then I gazed out the window, dreaming of Japanese babies, until the train pulled into Hiroshima Station.

Hiroshima is a city of water, shaped like a fan whose ribs are the six branches of the Ota River. Beyond the bombing, it's not a noteworthy place; visiting is like traveling to the United States and staying in Omaha. "I know you think Hiroshima is boring," Steven e-mailed, "but try to use your spare time to relax and think. Find a warm bench in the Peace Park and contemplate the future." I ignored him, stacking my days with back-to-back interviews.

Reporting in Hiroshima is a process of excavation. Part of it is the physical reality of the place; at any moment I could be walking on the bones of the dead, trampling on shards of past lives—broken crockery, a child's toy, a doctor's scalpel—that were long ago plowed under. Over fifty years after the bombing, ceramic buttons from junior high school uniforms still washed up on riverbanks rolling among smooth, round pebbles. Information, too, was buried under a sediment of fear, guilt, and shame, only sporadically, unexpectedly revealed. It was maddening for a can-do American like me, but *hibakusha* had reason to be wary. Even today, if a young man expresses interest in marrying a Hiroshima girl, his family may hire detectives to ensure she's not the descendant of survivors. The *hibakusha* who were willing to talk, who were more or less professional volunteers at the Peace Museum, were mostly childless, their relatives long dead. But they'd spoken to so many groups of tourists and

116

schoolchildren that their stories, as valuable as they were, tended to sound canned.

To find something less rehearsed I had to tread carefully, be referred by the right people. It was perilously easy to err. The Maidens, for instance, disliked one another. From the time they returned to Japan—sporting fashionable circle skirts, round-toed pumps, and a distinctly American swagger, their deformities diminished though by no means erased—they were dogged by reporters, stalked by paparazzi-style photographers. Often the coverage was brutal: so many died in the war, why should these women have received special treatment? Did the United States believe that patching up twenty-five girls was restitution for hundreds of thousands whom the Bomb maimed or killed? The criticism drove the women into semi-seclusion. They refused interviews and avoided one another. Three moved back to the States. Among those who remained, only Michiko Yamaoka talked to the press. "The others want to ignore what happened, to live quietly," she once told me. "I wanted the people of the world to know. I didn't want my experience to become a fairy tale."

I'd met Yamaoka on several previous trips to Japan, but during this visit, for the first time, she asked me to tea in her two-room home. Japanese generally socialize in public. Living quarters tend to be tiny; I've had friends for more than a decade whose apartments I've never seen. The invitation indicated a new level of trust. "I've lived here for forty-six years," she told me through an interpreter, as I removed my shoes in the dirt entryway. "It's falling down around me."

It was true—the walls, papered with news clippings and

117

thank-you drawings from schoolchildren around the world, were warped; the sitting room's straw tatami mats were patched and rotting. In one corner, next to the TV, was a photograph of Yamaoka's mother, Akino, dressed in a dark kimono, her white hair pulled tightly back. Each morning Yamaoka knelt before it, lit incense, rang a bell, and prayed. The shrine was surrounded by fruit, candles, and cups of coffee. "My mother loves coffee," Yamaoka explained, deliberately using the present tense. "I make her a cup every day."

Yamaoka's surgeries (twenty-seven during her eighteen months in America) restored mobility to her neck, which, because she'd looked up as the *Enola Gay* passed overhead, had melted into her left shoulder. They also gave her back the use of her fingers, which had fused as she raised her hands against the blast. Still, she fashioned much of her face in the mirror each morning, applying thick pancake makeup that couldn't fully cover her scars, drawing on an upper lip with pink lipstick, donning rose-tinted glasses to hide a drooping lower eyelid. She pointed to her cheek, to the patchwork of skin grafts culled from her belly. "If I gain weight, these get fat, too," she said, and laughed.

Despite her disfigurement, or maybe because of it, Yamaoka indulged in small vanities. She dyed her hair black to hide her age, took pains with her wardrobe. On this day she wore a jacket the color of daffodils over a blue skirt, and a gold band inlaid with onyx on one gnarled finger.

Yamaoka had asked me to her home for a reason. She wanted me to see the sole picture of her that survived the war. Taken in 1944, when she was fourteen, it showed a girl in a sailor-style school uniform with shoulder-length braids and a square jaw.

I scanned the face for some harbinger of what was to come, but there was none. She looked neither happy nor unhappy, merely ordinary.

I was drawn to Yamaoka's tale, as I was to Koko Kondo's, as a story of mothers and daughters, of limitless loyalty and a kind of profound love that I wondered if I would—if I *could*—ever feel myself.

Yamaoka's father had died when she was three. She spent her childhood shuttling between her mother, whom she described as a barmaid, and her wealthy aunt. "I remember taking English class in junior high," she said. "I remember learning"—she switched to heavily accented English—"*'this is a pen.'*" She laughed again and continued in Japanese. "But the next year the war with America broke out. Instead of learning English, we made bamboo spears and practiced lunging at scarecrows dressed in American soldiers' uniforms. It was supposed to prepare us if we were attacked."

Eventually the schools closed and everyone over twelve was forced to work for the war effort. Yamaoka was walking to her job at the phone company, clutching her lunch of two sweet potatoes in her hands, when the Bomb fell. She was fifteen. Knocked unconscious, she came to pinned under a boulder, the heat and crackle of fire approaching her. She screamed until her voice gave out, until she felt her mother touch her leg and cry "Michiko!" Then, in one of those legendary feats of maternal strength that are said to rise in crisis, Akino lifted the rock and dug her daughter out.

The girl was unrecognizable. Her face had inflated, the skin taut and cherry red. Strips of flesh hung from her arms. Over

119

the next few months mother and daughter were shunted among several makeshift infirmaries, none of which had doctors or medicine. Akino tended to Michiko the best she could, dressing her wounds with cooking oil when it was available, urine when it wasn't. At one point Akino tried to smother her daughter with a pillow to spare her further suffering. How to comprehend a despair so bottomless that to a mother murder felt like mercy? Another time, Yamaoka tried to drown herself. "I couldn't do it," she said solemnly, switching back to English. "I couldn't leave my mother."

Once Yamaoka could walk, the women returned to Hiroshima, squatting in a makeshift shack and scavenging metal to survive. Whenever she went outdoors, Yamaoka wore long sleeves, gloves, and a scarf pulled forward to hide her face. It didn't matter. Adults shouted at her on the streets to keep a distance. Children threw rocks and taunted her, calling her a monster. "I often sobbed to my mother that Japan took my face," she said. "Japan should give me my face back."

I fingered a picture of Yamaoka in 1955 squatting between two white children with toothy grins—a boy with his hair slicked back and a girl with curly pigtails and a plaid skirt. They were part of the family that hosted her in Connecticut while she was a Maiden. I tried to imagine her, a twenty-five-year-old who'd glimpsed hell but never seen the world, who hated leaving the house yet traveled to a country she still considered the enemy. What was it like to see the size of American homes, the surfeit of food, a washing machine, a refrigerator, an indoor toilet? To encounter forks and knives? "We had been taught table manners," she recalled. "Also how to take a Western-style bath, things like that. Even so, one girl washed her clothing in the toilet."

She returned to Hiroshima bolstered by American optimism and a scholarship to a trade school for seamstresses, but she never did pull herself and her mother out of poverty. Nor did she achieve the dream of the Maidens program: Yamaoka never married, never had a daughter of her own. She had a romance once, she confided, with a gentleman who lived in Tokyo. He wanted to wed, but she wouldn't leave her ailing mother. "I loved him," she said. "But I loved my mother more."

Chisa Tanimoto was warm-eyed, frail, and unable to answer many of my questions. I didn't care, because the instant I stepped into her living room, I was riveted by the infant boy lying swaddled in a teddy-bear-covered blanket. "Kenji-*desu*," Mrs. Tanimoto said, pointing at the baby. This is Kenji.

I asked if I could hold him. "*Konichiwa*, Ken-*chan*," I said, sliding a hand under his head. "*Ogenki desu ka?*" Hi, little Kenji. How are you? I shifted the baby to the crook of my arm, touched his pillow cheek, stroked his Sid Vicious hairdo. I gazed into his eyes, so dark that pupil and iris merged. How could I have missed the chance to be this child's mother? How could I have gotten here just weeks too late?

Perhaps sensing my desperation, Mrs. Tanimoto politely extricated Kenji and led me to a stack of scrapbooks about the Maidens. I leafed through, but kept one eye on the baby. *I could do this*, I thought, *I really could. I could adopt a Tanimoto orphan.* I didn't care where Kenji came from, who his father might be, or why his mother gave him up. I didn't care about his past. I wanted to be his future.

"You should've seen this baby," I said to Steven that afternoon on the phone. "He was so cute. I think you should write to Koko, too. She's impressed by you, it will look like we're more serious. And call Kent Nagano. See what he can do."

"That might be a good idea," Steven said, but his voice was guarded.

"What?" I asked. "What is it?"

"Nothing. But I'm not going to just say yes to all of this on the phone. We have to talk it through, decide if this is right for us."

"I think it is," I said. "I really do."

"And I'm not against it. But, Peg, you just had a miscarriage *last week*. And now you want to adopt? Doesn't that seem a little sudden?"

Perhaps my enthusiasm was just a hormonally driven illusion, I wasn't sure. But I was thirty-nine. We'd been trying to get pregnant for over three years. How much more was I willing to put myself through, my marriage through, to try to have a biological child? I thought about Kenji and, softer than the tuft of hair on his head, felt something rise in me once again—something close to hope.

Perhaps the Buddhists were on to something with the idea of *en*, or maybe we create omens, connect dots when we need to. Whatever the case, on this trip—my fourth to Hiroshima—I was inundated by stories of orphans. For years I'd been trying to talk to someone whose parents had died in the bombing, but the stigma proved impenetrable. Like my cab driver in Osaka, my interpreter in Hiroshima would nod when I asked her to set up meetings with orphans.

"*Muzukashi*," she would tell me. "It is difficult."

"I understand," I'd answer, "but please try." Instead, she would drag me to yet another appointment with a well-known storyteller from the Peace Museum. It took several visits before I realized that in Japan "It is difficult" actually means "When hell freezes over."

This time, after a number of false starts and subtle negotiations, my interpreter had found someone: a man, also named Yamaoka (no relation to Michiko), who owned a *minshuku*, a kind of family-run inn, about an hour outside of town. I asked my friend Yumi to join me—we could make a weekend out of it—but she politely declined. "I think this is something you should do yourself," she said, looking a little vague.

Again, I neglected to think like a Japanese. What she meant was, *minshukus* are for students and backpackers. They can be as cobwebbed and ooky as the Addams Family mansion. This one was dim and musty with a squinty-eyed stuffed boar mounted in the living room (Yamaoka had struck it with his car one night on the highway). My tatami mat room had neither furniture, heat, nor running water. There was an outhouse with a cold-water spigot across a breezeway, where the temperature was quickly sinking toward freezing. Some other time, or perhaps with Steven, this would've felt like an adventure. Right now it just felt primitive.

I joined Yamaoka, his wife, and an interpreter in the dining room. Yamaoka had prepared sukiyaki in a traditional cauldron that swung on a chain over a brick fire pit cut into the floor. I knelt beside him as he dished out a generous portion. The beef was thin-sliced and tender, the vegetables still slightly crunchy, the sauce fragrant. As the chill eased out of my body, my misgivings thawed, too. So did Yamaoka's. He was impressed that a *gaijin* wasn't afraid to eat sukiyaki the Japanese way, dipping each bite into a bowl of raw, beaten egg. By the time his wife brought our tea, he was laughing and making playful jokes at my expense. The light left his eyes, though, when he began the story that he'd never told a soul, that he'd kept inside for a half century.

Yamaoka was three when the Bomb killed his parents. A wealthy family took in his older sister, but didn't want a little boy. He moved in with his grandparents, aunts, and cousins in their ancestral home. "As long as my grandfather was alive it was fine," he recalled. "We were all treated equally. But when he died, the others began treating me like a servant. They made me live in a leaky shed in the backyard. I wasn't allowed to eat at the dinner table. My meals were their leftover bones and a yam. No rice. Then I washed their dishes outside in cold water. I was so malnourished that my belly distended. I had chilblains. And if I disobeyed, my grandmother whipped me. My teacher tried to convince them to let me go to an orphanage—it would've been better than what I endured—but that would've humiliated my grandmother, so she wouldn't do it.

"When I was ten, I tried to drown myself in the river, but before I could, a man grabbed me. 'Stop this foolish thing,' he said. 'If you kill yourself, who will take care of your parents' graves?' He'd been a soldier during the war and came back to find his whole family dead. He had his own problems, yet he worried about me. That kindness touched me."

I wish I could say that stories of cruelty at the hands of relatives were the exception among *hibakusha*, but they weren't. Children were abused or cast out. Wives who were left infertile because of the Bomb or malnutrition were tormented by their husbands' families. One survivor told me about her best friend, whose mother-in-law would rant, "You useless, sterile *hibakusha*. You've ruined my son's life. Why don't you kill yourself?" Eventually she did. Another survivor bore healthy sons, but her own radiation-induced infirmity became the source of harassment. A third gave birth to a disabled child, a birth trauma having nothing to do with the Bomb. That's not how her mother-in-law saw it. She harangued the young woman until she fled, leaving her two-year-old daughter behind.

Those stories shook me. I'm the wife of an only son of an only son from a Japanese American family. Steven is the last male to bear his surname. I'd had cancer and two miscarriages. But my mother-in-law cried with me, cried for me.

Yamaoka talked for hours, long after his wife went to bed. He seemed grateful for the opportunity and I was honored to listen. When I finally returned to the room I'd so carelessly dismissed, I reconsidered it through his eyes—how palatial, how secure it must feel. I unrolled my futon and changed, shivering, into my pajamas. In the old days, a neighbor would pace the streets about this time clapping two wooden blocks together, chanting, *"Hi no yo-jin"*—beware of fire—to remind everyone to put out their wood stoves. A peddler might wheel by with his udon soup cart crooning a melancholy tune, luring sleepy customers to have a last warm snack before turning in. Those small, comforting customs are all but gone. The locals accept that; it is only *gaijin* like me who wax nostalgic, who feel gypped out of something we wish we could have had.

In the morning, after a typical breakfast of miso soup and fish, Yamaoka drove me to the station, stopping to show me his town's main attraction: a hillside covered with thousands of irises, each in full bloom. We strolled along zigzagging paths, stopping to snap each other's picture. He came into my viewfinder's focus smiling proudly, arms swung wide, gesturing to the flowers, to the abundance of new life. This, too, was Hiroshima.

The only thing I could understand on the Japanese nightly newscast was the progress of the cherry blossoms, or *sakura*. Each evening, starting in mid-March, the weatherman pointed to a map showing where the blooms had already opened and forecasted where they would next appear. *Sakura* are considered the essence of Japan; tracking them was a near-hallowed task. The weatherman's voice was as earnest as if he were reporting on a tsunami.

This year *sakura* season felt like a personal affront. The delicate clouds of blossoms burst forth for a few fleeting days, a reminder to savor the present, to live in the now. The notion is called *wabi-sabi*: life, like the cherry blossom, is beautiful because of its impermanence, not in spite of it, more exquisite for the inevitability of loss. *Well*, I thought bitterly, *that and eight hundred yen would buy me a cup of green tea.*

A couple of hundred centuries ago, watching the blooms was

the sacred pastime of nobility. Now ubiquitous *ohanami*, or blossom viewings, are mostly an excuse to par-tay. The hot *ohanami* spot in Hiroshima was the Peace Park, a greenway built beneath the hypocenter of the explosion, filled with memorial shrines, a museum, and a burial mound. Despite its gravitas, it was a cheerful spot for an outing, with a canopy of pink and white blossoms lining the riverbanks. Junior executives staked their claims early in the morning, standing guard all day over blue plastic tarps. The rest of their groups would arrive at dusk, neatly removing their shoes before stepping on the mat and sitting in a perfect circle as if around an invisible table. They hibachi-grilled oysters, chicken, or hot dogs and snacked on *mochi* mixed with pink *sakura* petals and filled with sweet bean paste. Through it all, the sake and the beer flowed until revelers cut loose and began singing and dancing under the flowers. (Japanese drink more than anyone I have ever seen—women and men both. It's acceptable to go home blotto, puking in the streets and onto the subway tracks. My girlfriends in Tokyo considered my two-glass limit priggish. To them, drinking was a mark of modernity.)

My daytime schedule may have been jammed, but the evenings stretched out before me, long and blank. Mostly I wandered through a covered mall in the center of town, stopping to watch teenage boys with peroxide-streaked hair spin with joyless precision to an arcade game called *Dance Dance Revolution*. The night the *sakura* peaked, I broke that routine to shop for souvenirs at the baseball stadium where the Hiroshima Carp play. I strolled back through the park past the Peace Dome, the eerie, arcing skeleton of an exhibition hall that survived the bombing. I rambled along the river, checking out the festivities, listening to the laughter and the morale-boosting company cheers. No one noticed me. I felt formless, ectoplasmic, so unmoored that someone could have walked right through me, that I could have easily floated away. And it was a relief, a relief to drift untethered through a life that wasn't mine.

Back in my room, I wrote e-mails to friends telling them about the miscarriage. Given the stories of the *hibakusha* I'd heard all day, my own sorrows seemed trifling, a luxury of the fortunate. I wished that knowledge eased my pain. But if the *hibakusha* had taught me anything, it wasn't the irrelevance of grief, but indomitability despite it: they affirmed life in all of its horror and all of its beauty. That's what drew me back to Hiroshima over and over—admiration for the heroism of their humanity, for their cherry blossom hearts.

I opened an e-mail from Steven. He had phoned my parents to talk about the miscarriage and to tell them how much their support meant to us. They had begun to cry, though at first my dad tried to hold back. "When I got off the phone, I went out on the deck and wept like I should have when I was with you," he wrote. The letter depressed me: Steven was sitting alone under a cedar tree in Northern California, I was lying on a hotel bed in Hiroshima, both of us were crying. We hadn't shed a single mutual tear during his ten days in Tokyo. Were we so estranged that we could only mourn alone, that we could no longer cry together?

My window overlooked the panorama of the Peace Park. I could hear the corporate cheers slurring into slushy pop ballads at the *ohanami* gatherings below. Beyond them, I could make out the shadowy monuments to the dead: to the students of a girls' elementary school, to postal workers, to a neighborhood that had disappeared in an instant. The Peace Park was testament to the importance of remembering. Maybe that was the other reason I had returned here. I respected the need to make meaning out of life's randomness, out of its misfortunes big and small. As a writer, as a human being, I'd devoted my life to the power of story. I believed—for them, for me—that part of healing was in the telling. My own dilemma now was this: how could I memorialize someone who never really existed? Should I try to forget these babies, these nonbabies, that I'd lost? Could I, even if I wanted to?

8

JIZO SAVES

I heard the bells before I saw them, following the sound across the courtyard of Zojo-ji, a Buddhist temple in central Tokyo. There they were, lining a shady path: dozens of small figures of infants, each wearing a red crocheted cap and a red cloth bib, each with a bright-colored pinwheel spinning merrily in the breeze. Some had stone vases beside them filled with flowers or smoking sticks of incense. A few were surrounded by juice boxes or candy. A cap had slipped off one tiny head. Before replacing it, I stroked the bald stone skull, which felt surprisingly like a newborn's.

The statues were offerings to Jizo, a bodhisattva, or enlightened being, who (among other tasks) watches over miscarried and aborted fetuses as well as dead children. With their hands clasped in prayer, their closed eyes, and serene faces, they are both child and monk, both human and deity. I had seen Jizo shrines many times before. They're all over Japan, festive and not a little creepy. But this was different. I hadn't come as a tourist. I was here as a supplicant, my purse filled with toys, to make an offering on behalf of my own lost dream.

Just as I'd feared, my reentry to Tokyo had been bumpy. I kept up with my interviews, had dinner with friends, but my movements felt mechanical, my voice muffled. I tried to convince myself that getting pregnant again at all had been a victory. If I could do it twice, maybe I could do it a third time and it would finally stick. That was, however, an awfully tarnished silver lining to the miasma in my head.

I had never before considered that there was no ritual acknowledging miscarriage in Western culture, no Hallmark card to "celebrate the moment." There was certainly nothing in traditional Judaism, despite its scrupulous attention to the details of daily life. (My religion was mum on most matters of pregnancy and childbirth until, at least in the Reform and Conservative movements, female rabbis forced a change.) Christianity, too, has largely ignored the subject.

Without form, there is no content. So even in this era of compulsive confession, women don't speak openly of their losses. It was only now that I'd become one of them, that I'd begun to hear the stories, spoken in confidence, almost whispered. There were so many. My aunt. My grandmother. My sister-in-law. My friends. My editors. Women I'd known for years—sometimes my whole life—who had had this happen, sometimes over and over and over again but felt they couldn't, or shouldn't, mention it.

My shock and despair were, in part, a function of improved technology and medical care. In my mother's era a woman waited until she'd skipped at least two periods before visiting the doctor for a pregnancy test. If she didn't make it that long, she figured she was simply "late." It was less tempting, then, to inflate budding suspicions into full-blown fantasies—women often didn't even tell their husbands the news until the proverbial rabbit had died. Now prenatal care begins well prior to conception—for years I'd watched every milligram of caffeine, every glass of wine, every morsel of food, and forced down that daily horse pill of a prenatal vitamin. If I'd been in the United States, I could've peed on one of the new drugstore kit sticks and found out I was pregnant three days *before* I'd missed my period. As it was, at a tenuous five weeks gestation I'd already calculated my due date on a Web site, ogled pictures of "my baby's" development, and joined an Expecting Club on iVillage for November Mommies-to-Be. If the second IVF had taken, I would've taped that photograph of fertilized cells to the fridge. All of this encourages a mother-to-be to see the fetus as a person, at least in the psychological sense, at an ever-earlier stage. You tell friends. Names are bandied about. The baby feels real. Yet, if the pregnancy goes amiss, that personhood is abruptly revoked and you're supposed to act like nothing ever happened.

Maybe Americans suppress discussion of miscarriage because we don't like unhappy endings. We recoil from death. Better to push on, not to dwell. Personally, I was hypersensitive about being blamed for my loss, judged as "waiting too long," with the nasty implication that I got what I deserved. After all, I felt that way toward myself. But there was something else that held me back: my own pro-choice politics. I may have been able to distinguish psychological personhood from the biological or legal, yet that thread connecting me and my embryo had felt startlingly real, and at direct odds with everything I believed about when life begins. Nor had those beliefs—a complicated calculus of science, politics, and ethics—changed. I told myself that this hadn't been a person. It hadn't been a child. At the same time, I couldn't deny that it was something. Voicing my confusion, admitting that the bundle of cells I so adamantly called a zygote had felt to me like some sort of life, seemed like playing into the hands of the enemy.

So there I was, guilty and confused over my sadness, neither able to allow nor ignore it. Then I remembered Jizo. Of course the Buddhists would have a ritual for pregnancy loss; they're famously good at death. I phoned the mother of a Japanese friend to ask where I might make an offering. "I can't tell you," she responded. "You'll have to find the temple that is your *en*." That word was seriously beginning to bug me.

Eventually, a Japanese American friend back home suggested I try Zojo-ji, a fourteenth-century temple where the Tokugawa clan once worshiped that was legendary for its Jizo shrines. As it happened, the temple was a few blocks from Tokyo Tower, just a short walk from I-House. On my way there, I stopped at a toy store to buy an offering. What do you get for a child who will never be? I considered a plush Hello Kitty ball, then a rattle shaped like a tambourine, then a squeaky rubber An-pan Man—a popular superhero whose head is made of a sweet bean-filled pastry (which, when you think about it, is no more peculiar than a superhero who is a bat). This was no time to skimp, I decided, and scooped up all three.

"*Present-o?*" the salesclerk asked, reaching for some wrapping paper. I hesitated. Was it a gift? Not exactly.

"Is it for you?" she asked. I didn't know what to say.

"It's okay," I finally said. "I'll just take them like that."

I chose the long route to the temple, keeping my eye on Tokyo Tower, a red-and-white copy of the Eiffel Tower, as I triangulated the winding streets. The neighborhood was unusually quiet, full of low-slung old-fashioned buildings. I caught glimpses of dark interiors: an elderly woman selling bamboo shoots, something that looked like a homemade still, a motorbike parked inside a murky restaurant.

Finally I came across a temple gate and, assuming I'd arrived, stepped into a courtyard. Down a garden path I could see a contemporary marble statue holding a baby in one arm, a staff in the other. Two naked infants, their tushies lovingly carved, clutched the robes at its feet, glancing over their shoulders. At the base of the statue, someone had left a Kewpie doll.

"Is this Zojo-ji?" I asked an old woman who was sweeping up leaves. My Japanese was good enough to ask the question but not to understand her response. She motioned for me to wait, then fetched a monk, silver-haired in black robes. I was in the wrong place, he explained politely in English, then offered directions. For a moment I thought, *Why not just do it here?* I felt a flash of my familiar indecisiveness, then figured I'd stick to the plan, press on to Zojo-ji. As I left, I felt the tug of missed opportunity.

Another thing I'd never noticed: there is no word in English for a miscarried or aborted fetus. How better to bury a topic than to make it quite literally unspeakable? In Japanese it is *mizuko*, which is usually translated as "water child." Historically, Japanese Buddhists believed that existence flowed into a being slowly, like liquid. Children solidified only gradually over time and weren't considered to be fully in the human realm until they reached the age of seven. Similarly, leaving this world— returning to the primordial waters—was a process beginning at sixty with the celebration of a symbolic second birth. A *mizuko* lay somewhere along the continuum, in that liminal space between life and death but belonging to neither. True to the Buddhist belief in reincarnation, it was expected (and still is today) that Jizo would eventually guide the *mizuko* down another pathway into being. The idea behind the offering was to bid the *mizuko* farewell and wish it luck in the life it would have to come.

Jizo rituals were originally developed and practiced by women. There is evidence of centuries-old roadside shrines marking miscarriages, abortions, stillbirths, and the deaths of young children (particularly by infanticide, which was once widespread in Japan). But it wasn't until the late 1970s, when abortion rates peaked, that *mizuko kuyo*, the ritual of apology and remembrance, with its rows of Jizo statues, became commonplace. Abortion had been legalized in Japan after World War II, when food and resources were scarce; it was, then and now, viewed as a regrettable necessity—*shikataganai*. Rates remain high because of the Pill's inaccessibility, driven by fears about its safety and impact on the environment; fear that it encourages promiscuity and the spread of disease; and, not incidentally, because of pressure from doctors for whom abortion is lucrative. Even so, the procedure itself has been neither particularly controversial nor politicized. There is no real equivalent in Japan to our "pro-life" movement. The Japanese tend to be more tolerant of moral ambiguity, accepting both the inevitability of abortion and the idea that the *mizuko* is a form of life. I wondered how they could reconcile what seem to me such mutually exclusive viewpoints. But maybe that's the wrong question: maybe I should wonder why we can't.

About half of Japanese women perform *mizuko kuyo* after aborting. They may participate in a formal service, with a priest officiating, or make an informal offering. A woman may light a candle and say a prayer at a local temple. She may leave a handwritten message of apology on a wooden tablet. She may make an offering of food, drink, flowers, incense, or toys. The ritual may be a one-time act or it may be repeated monthly or annually. She may purchase her own Jizo statue (costing an average of about $500) or toss a handful of coins into a box at a roadside shrine. Sometimes couples perform *mizuko kuyo* together. If they already have children, they may bring them along to honor what is considered, in some sense, a departed sibling. The occasion becomes as much a reunion as a time to grieve. It struck me that *mizuko kuyo* contained elements that would both satisfy and disturb Americans on either side of the abortion debate: there is public recognition and spiritual acknowledgment that a potential life has been lost, remorse is expressed, yet there is no shame over having performed the act.

There was no mistaking Zojo-ji. It was a huge complex of epic buildings with a football field–size courtyard. I walked among the rows of *mizuko* Jizos searching for a spot to place my toys. Some of the babies' caps, which women crochet by hand, had rotted with age to just a few discolored strands. It was dank under the trees. A black cat eyed me from a ledge. It seemed a bad omen.

I wouldn't find out until months later, when I returned home, that there is another, darker side to *mizuko kuyo*. Over the past few decades, temples dedicated solely to the ritual have sprung up all over Japan, luring disciples by stressing the malevolent potential of the fetus: whether miscarried or aborted, it could become angry over being sent back. If not properly placated, it could actually seek revenge. In the mid-eighties, when *mizuko kuyo* was at its height, some entrepreneurial temples placed ominous advertisements in magazines: Are your children doing poorly in school? Are you falling ill more often than before? Has your family suffered a financial setback? Are you having nightmares? You must've neglected your *mizuko*.

Given the price tag on a Jizo statue, preying on women's fears is a profitable pursuit. At the Purple Cloud Mountain Temple, for instance, Japan's most famous contemporary *mizuko kuyo* site, thousands of Jizos dot the hillside. That gave me pause. Could something so coercive truly offer consolation? Then again, could thousands of Japanese women be so easily manipulated? They had to be getting something out of this. Perhaps like the ritual itself, in which conflicting realities exist without contradiction, both readings are true.

Standing amid the scores of Jizos at Zojo-ji, I considered: maybe I had found that little temple earlier for a reason. In retrospect, the garden had been cozy, the monk had been kind.

There were no rows of statues, no decomposing bonnets. It promised hope as well as comfort. I wanted to return but suddenly feared that the temple had been some kind of chimera, a Brigadoon that had already receded into the mists. More practically, I wasn't sure if I could find my way back.

Somehow I did, through a vague hunch and a good deal of blundering. The monk was dusting off a late-model Mercedes with two ostrich feather dusters. *So much for the mendicant's life*, I thought. For certain Buddhists, cleaning is enlightenment. I'd once read that polishing a wooden temple floor was like polishing the heart. I wondered if spiffing up a Mercedes counted.

He saw me and smiled. "Did you find it?"

"Yes," I said, "but I liked it here better. Is it okay if I stay awhile?"

"Do as you wish," he said. And I thought, *I'm trying*.

As it turned out, the statue at the temple was not Jizo; it was Kannon, goddess of compassion, to whom *mizuko kuyo* offerings are also sometimes made. Her androgynous face was tranquil but not warm. The expressions of the chubby stone babies at her feet were difficult to read. Had I surprised them? Distracted them? Was their backward glance a reminder that even as they played happily with the mother goddess, they would never forget the women whose bodies had been their hosts? Were they sad? Or was I projecting my own sorrow, now a gnawing presence in my stomach, onto them? I focused on the reassuring image of the Kewpie doll that had been placed there, the happy and dimpled Western baby. It seemed less ambiguous.

As I arranged my offering at Kannon's feet, a distant bell tinkled, similar to the sound of the pinwheels. I looked up, startled.

It stopped a second later and didn't start again. I am a cynic by nature, with a journalist's skeptical heart. But increasingly I was in the mood to believe.

My toys looked right surrounding Kewpie, the whole place a little cheerier. I liked them there. I liked the delicate lavender bushes surrounding me in the garden, the wild irises with their ruffled edges, the azaleas, the fleabane and camellias. They were the same plants as in my yard back in California. Crows cawed—the perpetual soundtrack of Tokyo—and traffic passed in a steady hum. Still, for that city it was a meditative spot. I relaxed, at last. Maybe my *en* was finally back on track.

Twilight was falling, and the garden turned cold. I clapped my hands three times, as one is supposed to at shrines, and backed away, gazing once more at the impassive marble face. Was there kindness there?

The temple grounds were empty. The monk in his Mercedes, the lady sweeping leaves were both gone. I rummaged in my purse for an envelope and five thousand yen—about forty dollars. "To the monk I met at 5 P.M. from the foreign woman looking for Zojo-ji," I wrote. "Could you please chant a lotus sutra for me and my *mizuko?* Thank you."

I slipped it under the door. I didn't know whether it was appropriate or whether he would do it. But there were so many things I couldn't know. Maybe learning to live with the question marks—recognizing that closure does not always occur—was all I could do, at least for now. I hadn't expected, coming from a world that fights to see life's beginnings in black and white, to be so comforted by a shade of gray. Yet the notion of the water child made sense to me. What I'd experienced had not been a full life, nor was it a full death, but it was a real loss. Maybe my *mizuko* would come back to me more fully another time, or maybe it would find someone else. Surprisingly, even that thought was solace. I wasn't exactly at peace as I left the temple—grief is not so simply dispensed with—but I felt a little easier. I had done something to commemorate this event; I'd said good-bye. I was grateful to have had that chance.

As I headed back to I-House, the sky deepened from peach to salmon to lavender, and motorists switched on their headlights. The bittersweet smell of fish grilled with soy sauce—which had revolted me when I was pregnant—permeated the air. I breathed it in deeply. I decided to try a new route through the unnamed back streets, not sure of the direction, but trusting, for the first time since arriving here, that eventually I would find a way home.

9

PUT THE LIME IN
THE COCONUT

———————

Yu Wan Chang was unhappy with the state of my tongue. There was a crack running down its middle and it was coated in white. These are bad signs. In traditional Chinese medicine, each segment of the tongue corresponds to a part of the body— the tip to the lungs, the base to the bladder, and so forth. So you can understand Dr. Chang's dismay: my tongue was telling her that I was a mess.

This was not news to me. In the month since returning from Japan, I'd become so tightly wrapped I fairly vibrated, my sadness and anger surfacing in unpredictable bursts. I began avoiding social situations, afraid that if someone asked me a personal question like, say, "How are you?" I'd actually tell her. Before, I could channel my energy into fertility treatments. Plus, I could always comfort myself with worst-case scenarios: I didn't get pregnant on Clomid, but neither did my sister-in-law, and she went on to have three children; I didn't produce many follicles during IVF, but neither did Kristin, and she went on to have twins; I had a miscarriage, sure, but so did a friend who was now the mother of four. But I had run out of Cinderella stories.

"It feels so unfair," I complained to Steven. "Everyone else has a baby. I've been through so much—I should get to have one, too."

"You're wrong," he said. "It's not unfair. Unfair is when my friend Lynn died at forty-two. Unfair is that her daughter was only three at the time. This is unfortunate, but it's not unfair. You'd never say that you deserve to have a writing project go well because the last one went badly. It's the same thing. Life is not quid pro quo."

"It's not the same to me," I sulked. "I'm starting to feel like a chronically unlucky person."

"That's too bad," he replied, his face hard. "It really is."

A few minutes later, he apologized. "I'm sorry to be so harsh. Sometimes I snap at you when I'm mad at myself. All of a sudden I feel like everywhere I go, all I notice is children. I resent it. I'm embarrassed by how easily I'm affected by that feeling of *Why can't I have what everyone else has?* It feels pathetic."

Then I talked to my friend Susannah in Los Angeles. She'd had trouble conceiving, too, but after a few miserable months on the devil Clomid she'd switched to acupuncture and herbs. Four weeks later she was pregnant. Her daughter, Olivia, was born the same month my first baby had been due. I had taped a picture of her to my refrigerator dressed as Dorothy in blue gingham for Halloween, clutching a plastic pumpkin, her gleeful smile a carbon copy of her mother's. Susannah was pregnant again—this time with a boy—and again due the same month I would have been. I gritted my teeth and congratulated her.

"It was the acupuncturist," she confided. This time she hadn't messed around; she'd gone to him right away. "I think Western medicine is great for trauma, like a car wreck or a broken leg, but for something systemic, I'd try Chinese medicine first."

Susannah is from old New England stock; her family name graces foundations, museums, a university. She's the product of three generations of physicians. I have never known her to wear patchouli or attend Burning Man. If she said pins got her pregnant, I was inclined to believe her.

"At least it might help you relax," Steven said when I brought up the idea. "Besides, it's cheaper than therapy. If you keep running at this level of stress, you're going to have a breakdown—that's going to cost a lot more."

Dr. Chang had a loving, almost yielding presence. A woman of indeterminate age—I'd put her anywhere between forty and seventy—she had a shy smile and hair pulled into a flyaway bun. She'd taught gynecology at a Chinese medical school before coming to Texas in the 1980s to do research on IVF. Now she was an instructor at the American College of Traditional Chinese Medicine in San Francisco. With that pedigree, she had to know what she was doing, even if the walls of her waiting room were covered in plastic philodendron vines, even if the questions she asked seemed arbitrary. Was I perpetually thirsty? Did I have headaches? Were my feet cold? She probed for details about my bowel movements and urination. Did I bruise easily? (Yes.) Was my skin dry? Were my nails brittle?

Was I an insomniac? (Yes, yes, yes—but what the heck did all that have to do with fertility?)

"How is your sexual energy?" she asked.

"I've been trying to get pregnant for three and a half years," I deadpanned. "I have no sexual energy."

She held my wrists, her hands warm and papery. "Hmm," she said, frowning. "Small pulse."

"Is that bad?"

She shrugged her shoulders. "It's a sign of liver *qi* stagnation."

Qi (pronounced "chee"), she explained, is the vital energy that acupuncturists believe moves through the body along meridians stimulating the organs. When it's out of whack you get sick, you get infertile, you get a white tongue. In my case, sluggish *qi* was apparently keeping blood from my uterus, making it difficult to get or stay pregnant. That seemed as plausible as anything else I'd heard.

"Can you help me?" I asked.

"You only have one ovary," she hedged, "so your chances are lower than other people's, but you got pregnant naturally twice so that's a good sign."

I pushed a little harder. "Do you have any data on your success rates?"

Dr. Chang pulled out an article from a file on her desk. Published in the jolly-sounding *Fertility and Sterility* journal, it described a randomized trial of 160 women undergoing IVF. Half had one acupuncture treatment immediately before and after their embryo transfer. Half didn't. Thirty-four of the first group were pregnant six weeks later versus only 21 of the control group. Impressive, but that didn't necessarily mean that months—

or years—of weekly needlings would affect my odds of getting pregnant naturally. Later I would scour the Internet for something more concrete. Although I found plenty of assertions on acupuncturist's sites such as "turning back the biological clock is indeed possible," they offered no scientific proof that this was so. Most referenced the same study Dr. Chang had, similarly extrapolating across the board, claiming that traditional Chinese medicine "increased pregnancy rates by over 50 percent."

There's something about acupuncture that begs one to suspend disbelief. Cancer patients I knew, women who had read every study on an FDA-approved drug before agreeing to take it, willingly downed Chinese herbs without asking what they were or what harm they might do. It didn't really matter; for most of us the treatments were less about efficacy than mystery, yet another source of that narcotic high of hope. Even in the introduction to Dr. Chang's own self-published book a former patient admitted, "My husband, the physician, believes that Chinese medicine is only a placebo, but *I don't care* [emphasis mine] because it worked for us and we are very, very happy." I understood that impulse. I felt so broken, my well-being so battered—who was going to give me an Rx for that?

While I finished reading, Dr. Chang filed a stack of folders. A picture of a woman with a fuzzy-headed newborn accidentally slid out of one. "She was forty years old," Dr. Chang said before tucking it away. "She tried to get pregnant many times and had multiple miscarriages before she came to me. Just like you. Now she has a baby."

Maybe it wasn't the double-blind evidence I was looking for, but what did I have to lose? Besides (all together now),

What if this worked? What if it was the only way I could have a baby?

"Her husband had a low sperm count," Dr. Chang added, as she led me back to a small room. "I also strengthened his sperm. It's very important that your husband come in to see me, too." I nodded earnestly, wondering how I'd ever convince Steven of that.

After shucking my shoes, socks, and jeans, I lay down on a massage table under the warming glow of several heat lamps. Dr. Chang pressed tiny needles, the width of a child's hair, into my shins, on either side of my pelvis, in my forehead, and in the webbing between my thumb and forefinger. Once, when she pushed a needle in too deeply, a shock shot up my leg, but mostly I felt nothing. She placed several more needles along the rims of my ears.

"Why there?" I asked.

"In Chinese medicine the ear represents an inverted fetus."

Eww. Sorry I asked.

For free, she slid a final needle into what she called the Happiness Point on the top of my head. Then she told me not to move (Would you if you were a human pin cushion?) and placed a hotel call bell in my hand. "Ring if you need anything," she said. "Otherwise, rest."

I looked around the room as best I could without turning my head. There was a container of multicolored fine-toothed combs, the kind you'd find in a 1950s barbershop, affixed to a mirror on one wall. Underneath, a handwritten sign invited, PLEASE TAKE ONE. I wondered if anyone ever had. I stared out the window at a sliver of sky and listened to the white noise of downtown San Francisco seventeen floors below. The heat lamps felt good on my skin.

A half hour later Dr. Chang touched my shoulder. "You fell asleep," she said softly. The needles in my ears had worked free and become tangled in my curls—I guess the founders of Chinese medicine hadn't reckoned on treating Brillo-headed Jewish girls. She unwound them, then handed me a plastic bottle of coarse-grained brown powder, instructing me to mix three spoonfuls into a cup of hot water twice a day.

I unscrewed the cap and took a whiff; it smelled like feet.

Dr. Chang chuckled. "You get used to it," she said.

A TV commercial from my childhood flashed through my mind, the one in which the "ancient Chinese secret" of a laundry owner named Mr. Lee was unmasked as Calgon. For all I knew, I was signing on to drink Miracle-Gro. On the other hand, injecting hamster ovaries and nuns' urine hadn't done the trick. And at a hundred dollars a crack, Dr. Chang's treatments were a bargain, cheaper than anything I'd tried since Clomid. Science had done me no favors; maybe pseudoscience could. I made another appointment.

That night I asked Steven about the combs.

"It's a Chinese tradition to give a person something when you take something from them, like money."

"She's already giving me something—her services."

He shrugged. "Yeah, well I'm not Chinese, am I? Don't ask me."

"She wants you to go, too," I said, tentatively. To my surprise, he was game. He, after all, was jonesing for hope himself. He wanted to believe that if he only did what I asked, he could make me happy, that he could get his wife and his marriage back. At the very least, he would tell me later, he hoped he could turn the appointments into dates together in the city; we could go shopping in Union Square afterward or share our favorite beet and fennel salad at Scala's Bistro around the corner.

"I don't know about taking herbs, though," he said. "I think that's a racket. I'm not saying they're harmful, but I don't think they'll get us pregnant. And they taste like dirt."

Maybe so, I thought as I wound my arms around him, *but honestly, in every relationship, doesn't one have to eat a little dirt?*

This time we saw the heartbeat, a pale, blurry tic-tac pulsing against the darkness of my belly. There was a heart inside me—someone else's heart. I was seven weeks pregnant and as terrified as I was awed.

Dr. Chang nodded when I told her, as if she knew this would happen. "See, only four treatments," she boasted. She said her herbs would prevent another miscarriage; I decided to forget that I'd heard that one before.

Eight weeks. Risa's practice now had its own ultrasound machine. I closed my eyes as she slid the wand across my stomach, the blood pounding in my ears. "Be there," I silently begged. "Please be there." It was—bigger, stronger, though still little more than a smudge of light.

"Hello, Kai," I said, barely above a whisper.

I careened between East and West, seeking some kind of guarantee from either side. Dr. Chang claimed she could cure the morning sickness that had hit me as virulently as in my first pregnancy. She couldn't. There were days, after my seventh face-to-face with the toilet bowl, when I thought I couldn't take it anymore. I prayed for the pregnancy to end, then quickly assured God I was just kidding. Sort of. Risa, meanwhile, ordered me hooked up to an IV and prescribed antinausea drugs. They didn't help much either, though at least they knocked me out for most of the day. Dr. Chang warned me to avoid air travel during the first trimester; Risa said it probably made no difference. I wasn't taking any chances: I postponed magazine assignments, canceled speaking engagements. I kept my fingers crossed, but not my legs, in case, as I'd read somewhere, that cut off circulation to my uterus.

Nine weeks. Risa squinted at the screen. "I'm not seeing anything," she said slowly. I began to shake. Steven stroked my arm, steadying. "Don't jump to conclusions," she continued. "This isn't a powerful machine." It was six o'clock on a Friday afternoon. She touched my knee. "I'm calling the hospital. I'm going to get them to squeeze you in. I'm not letting you wait all weekend like this."

"But we saw a heartbeat," I said to Steven, as we hurried to the car. "It was there. It can't just go away, can it?"

It could. When the radiologist told us, I thanked him calmly. Then, as we walked through the hospital lobby, my knees buckled. Steven caught me, kept me from crumpling. I keened. I wailed. I didn't care that there were people walking by, that an abundantly pregnant girl, no older than sixteen, was gawking at me. *Why her*, I thought, *and not me?* I sobbed myself dry. This was not like the first time. It was not even like the second. Anyone can tell you, three strikes and you're out.

"I know," Steven murmured as I wept. "I know it's hard." He

didn't tell me it would be all right. He didn't say that we'd be okay. How could he?

Monday morning, before the D&C, Risa pressed my hand. "Give this woman some really good drugs," she told the anesthesiologist. "She's been through a lot. Too much." I stared at the ceiling as the vacuum sucked at my womb, willing myself into the tiny holes of the soundproofing. The first time, I'd been in shock. The second, I'd been unconscious. This time I was all there—I was all there, and it hurt.

I found out later that if the baby had lived, a chromosomal abnormality would've left it severely retarded, with a defective heart and ghastly facial and limb deformities. So yes, nature did her job; nature did me a favor. That didn't make the loss less devastating.

I also found out that he was indeed a boy. That was something I didn't want to know.

Dr. Chang seemed to sense when my faith was flagging, when I wearied of making the weekly haul into the city. On those days she'd already have a picture in hand when I arrived. "See," she'd say. "She was your age, came to me for a year, and now she has a baby." Once, when another photo "accidentally" slipped out of a file I even saw the patients' names. The husband was someone I knew; we had been editors at the same magazine in New York in the 1980s when he'd been married to his first wife. I hadn't seen him in at least fifteen years, didn't know he'd moved to the Bay Area. I was fairly certain he wouldn't want me privy to the details of his sperm count. The photos were such a transparent manipulation, yet I fell for it every time. And how different was it, really, than the walls of baby names in the fertility clinics, the burbling infants on their Web sites, the souvenir snapshots of cells, or three-ringed binders overflowing with birth announcements and holiday cheer? Everyone used their successes to woo our aching hearts. Everyone coerced and equivocated—the doctors, the acupuncturists, the Yoga for Fertility instructors. They all dangled something just shy of a promise in front of us, then yanked it out of reach.

In the four years that I'd been trying to get pregnant, the number of annual IVF attempts had shot up by 78 percent; Americans were spending over 2.7 billion dollars a year pursuing fertility treatments. Bookstores devoted entire sections to volumes implying they could get you pregnant (and that you won't conceive without them). In one, *Six Steps to Increased Fertility*, a trio from the Harvard Medical School faculty wrote that infertile women report the same levels of anxiety and depression as cancer patients. (Amateurs, I scoffed—what about those of us who've had both?) They also claimed, like Dr. Chang, that stress hampers conception. That, for me, was where this alternative stuff got dodgy; it always seemed to find a way to blame you for your malady, putting the locus of the problem in your head rather than your body as surely as did comments like "Just relax," "Take a vacation," or, as one acquaintance suggested, "Why don't you just take a bottle of wine to bed and enjoy your husband."

I recalled best-selling author Louise Hay, who maintained that breast cancer was caused by "deep-seated resentment," and Yale Medical School professor Bernie Siegel, who claimed, "Happy people generally don't get sick." Now, I discovered,

Chinese medicine believed that my infertility was due to an "inner psychological frustration about having and raising children." If that were the case, why were there ever unwanted babies? What's more, I'd never seen anything blaming men for sperm defects.

The Harvard docs took pains to say that anxiety is the by-product, not the cause, of infertility; yet if stress discourages pregnancy, and you've let infertility stress you out, what is a girl supposed to think? Especially when the book breathlessly repeats the italicized statistic that their "*Mind/Body program has an over 30 percent success rate for conception.*" This had to be my fault, didn't it? My education, my social status, the era in which I lived, had all taught me I could be anything I wanted to be, do anything I wanted to do, be mistress of my fate. Wasn't the corollary, then, that I also caused my own misfortune?

People in pain are so vulnerable, such easy marks. We're desperate for reasons, for a sense of control, even if it means incriminating ourselves. A friend noticed that when referring to the miscarriages I would say I'd had two, plus a partial molar pregnancy. "Why do you differentiate that way?" she asked.

"I don't know," I said, although, in truth, I did. Because the first one, the partial molar pregnancy, was due to a sperm abnormality. It had nothing do with my body, my choices, my ambivalence, my age. Because I didn't blame myself for it. Because it didn't choke me with guilt.

I had to admit that despite my fear of becoming one of those people who speaks in a carefully modulated voice, my thermonuclear anxiety was exhausting me. I wasn't sure I fully bought the stress-infertility connection (Wouldn't it follow, then, that only happy women got pregnant easily?), but even I could see I needed to ratchet it down a smidge. The acupuncture was one step. The Harvard crew suggested replacing negative thoughts—"I'll never have a baby"—with positive ones—"I'm doing everything I can to get pregnant." They also advised daily meditation. So I tried. I did. I set a timer for nine minutes, settled myself into a chair, and concentrated on my breath. After three minutes I opened one eye to check the clock. After six minutes, my back hurt. After seven, I decided a more effective relaxation technique would be vegging out with a can of Pringles in front of the Style Network.

That October, five months into our treatment, Steven refused to go back to Dr. Chang. It was too expensive, he claimed. Anyway, he didn't have time; he was spending the fall shooting a new film in Santa Cruz, about an hour south of Berkeley when the traffic is clear (which it never is). He had set up shop in a hotel there, and I would come down to visit on weekends and when I was ovulating. "I can't make a special trip to the city every week anymore," he said one afternoon. "I have a life. I have a job. You can keep doing it, but I'm done. It's enough. Besides, I'm tired of walking by people's gardens, seeing the dead leaves, and wondering, 'Is that what I'm eating?'"

It was once again Indian summer, when Northern California is bleached blond and dry. It hadn't rained since April; our morning walk through the hills behind Steven's hotel left our shoes covered in dust. At the trailhead a sign instructed us on how to fend off a mountain lion: stand erect, face forward, make eye contact, speak in a brave voice—and if it does attack, fight back. I wished I could follow that advice in the rest of my life.

"I saw one yesterday morning," Steven said, casually.

"Oh my God! A mountain lion? What did you do?"

He shook his head. "Nothing. I watched it for a while, then kept going."

That composure, I thought, was the essential difference between him and me. For the rest of our walk, I waved my arms over my head trying to make myself look larger and more fierce, just in case. If nothing else, it kept the cougars laughing too hard to pounce.

Afterward we had coffee on a veranda overlooking the sweep of the Santa Cruz mountains. "I've made a decision," Steven said. "I'll only keep trying to get pregnant if you stop caring."

Stop caring? He might as well have told me to stop breathing.

"I'm tired of putting my life on hold," he continued. "I'm tired of basing everything on your menstrual cycle. I'm tired of *knowing* about your menstrual cycle. Your first question when I told you I'd be shooting down here wasn't to ask about the project, it was about how it would affect your cycle. If that's what you care about—if it's *all* you care about, if you don't care about what I'm doing—then we're not having a relationship anymore."

"But I can't just not care," I said. "And I don't stand around watching mountain lions. I'm not you."

He looked out at the view, shaking his head. "I don't know how to say it any other way, Peg. *I can't do this.* You're destroying our marriage. I love you as much as I always have. I feel it all the time when I'm away from you, but then I call to see how you are, to have a laugh and share our day, and you're not my partner anymore. You pretend to talk about normal things, but I can tell you're thinking about fertility the whole time. You're this angry, bitter person fixated on having a baby. And—I'm not saying it's going to happen—but if someone else came along and cared about me and wanted to hear what I had to say, I'd be vulnerable. I want you to know that. It wouldn't be one of those things where you could say, 'We were getting along so well. I have no idea why this happened.' I'm not threatening you, but I want you to be aware."

I wish I could say that Steven's warning, his pleading, brought me to my senses, made me realize how sorely I'd neglected him. But perversely, it was my very faith in his commitment to our relationship that had allowed me to abuse it. I had convinced myself that we'd survive the damage I was inflicting, that it was reversible, even necessary. I would make it up to him later, after we had a baby. Right now, I needed him to want what I wanted. And if I couldn't have that, I needed him to *do* what I wanted. My husband was telling me straight out that as much as he loved me, he wasn't sure he could stay in our marriage. And my only response was to think, "*Now* how do I get him to have sex with me?"

The solution seemed obvious: I had to lie. I took his hand in both of mine and gazed deeply into his aggrieved eyes. "Okay, it's a deal. I'll try to stop caring."

"*Trying* isn't good enough. You've said that before."

I nodded. "I'll *stop* caring. I will. And I won't bug you about going to Dr. Chang anymore.

"But if I bring it down here," I added, "will you please keep drinking the dirt?"

* * *

155

Some people believe adopting will get them pregnant. They begin the process secretly thinking they won't have to go through with it, that filling out the forms will jump-start their bodies. I knew that was absurd. Adopting won't get you pregnant, buying a dog will. My brother and sister-in-law conceived their first daughter shortly after bringing home a rambunctious golden Lab (whom they eventually sent to a farm—honestly).

I didn't want a dog solely for its thermaturgic properties, though. I was also lonely, deeply lonely. Steven was immersed in his film, away much of the time. My friends were busy with their children. I worked alone in my house, in a hilly neighborhood with no sidewalks. There were days when the only other mammal I saw was the squirrel who buried nuts in the potted plants on our back deck. A dog would keep me company, I reasoned. It would be something to take care of, to nurture. Steven was agreeable, too, relieved that I was interested in something besides baby making.

I did know that a dog wasn't a child, though that, apparently, is not a commonly shared observation in Berkeley. In a town of people who have a tendency to be a mite zealous, the dog people are extreme. They successfully lobbied for an ordinance forbidding citizens to *own* pets—we can't even call them pets. We must refer to ourselves as the "guardians" of our "animal companions." What's more, purebreds are as anathema as SUVs: the only correct choice is a rescue dog, to discourage overpopulation. In theory, we agreed, but four visits to a local no-kill shelter—which housed a collection of pit bull and Doberman mixes in cement and chain-link cages— changed our minds. We quickly learned that "exuberant" was code for "aggressive," and "energy to spare" meant "kiss your shoes good-bye."

We also tried a local animal sanctuary that places its dogs with "foster parents" until a "forever family" can be found. At their weekly event on an upscale shopping street, we fell in love with a sweet-eyed, silk-furred border collie mix. A sign nearby said he'd been "adopted" once, but was quickly returned.

"Could I get some information about the dog?" I asked a volunteer.

She looked irritated. "What kind of information?"

"Like the reason he was returned?" She sighed as if I were trying her patience.

"He bit the vet, okay? But it was only because the vet grabbed him under his ribs."

"He *bit* someone?"

"Only because he grabbed him under his ribs," she repeated, as if I were slow-witted. "You normally wouldn't do that."

"I think we'll pass," I said. She glared at us until we walked away.

Around that time a baby panic spread among educated, urban young women, the kind who typically prized Manolo pumps over Madelas. Two things, so to speak, egged it on: the American Society for Reproductive Medicine (ASRM) launched a "public service campaign," plastering buses in major cities with pictures of an hourglass-shaped baby bottle, the milk of time running out. In block capital letters, the tagline screamed, ADVANCING AGE DECREASES YOUR ABILITY TO HAVE CHILDREN. Take *that* with your morning coffee, Carrie Bradshaw. Simultaneously, economist

Sylvia Ann Hewlett's *Creating a Life: Professional Women and the Quest for Children* was published to a media blitz that would be the envy of J. K. Rowling. Hewlett reported that "ultra-achieving" women in their forties and fifties were suffering a "crisis of childlessness" brought on not only by the brutal demands of the workplace, but also by the willful ignorance of their own biological clocks. As a result, they were crippled by regret. The book made *60 Minutes* and the covers of *Time* and *New York Magazine*. (The ASRM campaign, meanwhile, made the cover of *Newsweek*.) It was promoted on *Today*, *Good Morning America*, *The View*, and even the *NBC Nightly News*. It was debated on the editorial pages of both the *Los Angeles Times* and the *New York Times*. For months, wherever young women turned, they encountered Hewlett's Chicken Little natalism, her exhortations to blunt their ambitions, hook a husband, and get pregnant pronto, or risk being as bereft as their older sisters.

It was because of this wrinkle in the zeitgeist—and because *Flux*, my second book had been about women's life choices—that I got the Call: the one that all authors dream of, the one that could lift us from obscurity to riches. Be still my beating heart—it was *Oprah*. "We've been trying to track you down for days," her producer scolded. "We're looking for someone who can defend women in their forties who don't have children. We thought given your work you might be able to do that."

Of course I could. It wasn't like I didn't have a response to Hewlett. I could have pointed out that all the babies in the world wouldn't compensate for a middling marriage and a second-rate job. I could have questioned why Hewlett didn't discuss men's roles (beyond their aversion to marrying profession-ally successful women). I could have challenged the ASRM to restructure medical training to make it easier for women in their own field to heed their message. I might have attacked the gap-ing flaws in Hewlett's research or trotted out the zillions of stud-ies showing that childless women are as happy as mothers. If I were feeling snarky, I might have even gotten personal: Hewlett gave birth to her *fifth* child at age *fifty-one* after four years of in-fertility treatments. Mightn't that indicate a perspective on motherhood that was, I don't know, just a wee bit . . . warped?

But then again, so was my own. I knew the correct, the feminist—hell, the *reasonable*—response, but I no longer be-lieved it. Not in my heart. I felt like the poster child for Hewlett's thesis, the midlife professional who'd badly miscalculated, who found out too late that her accomplishments were meaningless compared to motherhood. I no longer knew how to find my way back to my marriage unless I was pregnant. I needed a baby to restore faith in my defective body, heal my wounded sexuality, assuage my grief, relieve my feelings of failure—to make me whole again. At one time, I would have told a woman like me that childlessness was not her problem; it was her inability to recognize the value in all that she had, in all that she'd built for herself. But I had become the woman I once pitied, the one who was too easily swayed by gross oversimplifications that collapsed all of life's complexities into the convenient box of "waited too long." My situation, like most women's, was so much more com-plicated than that, but who cared? My sense of failure infected every corner of my life, including my former refuge: my work. Even when writing about something unrelated to motherhood,

I no longer trusted my instincts, second-guessed my observations. If I couldn't handle "How are you?" how could I expect, on national TV, to weather "Do you regret not having children?" How could I defend my choices when I was questioning everything I'd ever believed, everything I'd valued? Who was I to act as an expert on contemporary womanhood when my own life was a mess? Infertility had rocked me to my core.

So, even as my publisher's publicist bombarded the producer with press releases and clippings, I did the one thing I was sure would scotch my shot of being on the show. "I'd love to do it," I told her. "As long as I don't have to talk about anything personal."

I pretended to be disappointed when she e-mailed me a few days later to say they had gone another way, but secretly I was relieved.

In lieu of a dog, I began courting a stray tabby cat who lurked near my office door, coaxing her closer with saucers of milk. Soon she would approach me eagerly in the morning, purring and jumping on my lap while I wrote.

"Do we have a cat?" Steven asked on a weekend home from Santa Cruz.

"Maybe," I said, as she wound around his legs. "She's pretty sweet. And she needs a home."

I christened her Kitkat, a non-name reflecting the tenuousness of my claim. One afternoon as I petted her in my driveway, a little girl walked by with her father. "Rio!" She squealed.

"Oh," I said, my heart sinking. "Is this your cat?"

"Yes," she said, firmly. Her father, standing behind her, shook his head. "She likes to *say* it's her cat; it's a stray that hangs around our yard sometimes."

Hmph, I thought. *If that girl thinks she's wrestling my cat away, she has another thing coming.* As soon as they were out of sight, I went inside for a can of tuna. Rio-shmio. This was Kitkat.

I gave Kitkat the run of the house, but within a week she'd turned from a welcome guest into the boor who stays too long. She howled if I didn't let her in as soon as I woke up each morning. She bit when I tried to remove the burrs from her coat. She scratched up the dining room chairs. Not only that, she made me sneeze. I'm not usually allergic to cats, but I was to this one. "I don't think I can keep her," I wheezed to Steven on the phone, during one of a string of asthma attacks.

I left a dish of cat food outside—I didn't want to cut her off completely—but kept my door closed. She wasn't having it. She began stalking me, circling the perimeter of the house trying to figure out which door I was nearest. Then she'd stand on her hind legs and scratch frantically. I closed the blinds, put in earplugs. Nothing helped. My worst fear was being realized: I was trapped by the very being I'd tried to nurture, a prisoner in my own home. That's when she began to mewl, sounding exactly like a crying baby. I fled the premises and began working in a café.

I went back to looking for a dog, if only to chase that infernal cat away. Instead of infertility sites, I swapped one obsession for another, combing the Web for information on specific breeds. I dragged Steven to dog shows to meet sellers. After a flirtation with miniature Australian shepards, I homed in on Portuguese water dogs, which don't shed and look like cuter standard poodles. One hitch: a Porty puppy cost eight hundred bucks—for that amount, the "animal companion" better be a good conversationalist. What's more, the breeders I met had some serious boundary issues. One reserved the right to repossess a dog if I couldn't prove I'd taken it to obedience classes. Another expected to be able to inspect my house unannounced at *any time for the life of the dog* to make sure it was being properly treated. A third would forbid me to give the dog away and wanted notification whenever I moved or changed my e-mail address. Getting a dog began to seem as difficult as having a baby. I gave up the search.

Late in October I heard a voice on my office message machine. "Hello, this is Koko Tanimoto Kondo. I am calling from Japan." I reached for it, then stopped, my hand poised midair. There could only be one reason for Koko to phone me, and I didn't want to hear it. "Could you please call me as soon as possible?" I waited until she hung up, then I hit the delete button.

It had been over six months since Koko and I had met. In that time I'd made only one follow-up phone call, to an agency in San Francisco that facilitated international adoption. They'd sent me a manila envelope bulging with information, including an astonishingly intrusive list of forty-three questions required for the social worker's clearance. "Briefly comment on the relationship of your parents (a) to each other, (b) with you, and (c) with your partner." *Briefly?* "Describe your adolescence." "Comment on your relationship and on any previous significant relationships or marriages." I could write entire books on each of those topics. I wanted to respond with my own inquiry: *Why are potential adoptive parents—most of whom have already struggled*

*for years to conceive—subject to such intense scrutiny when most
people become parents because the condom breaks?*

I lay the form on a corner of my desk, where it was quickly
buried under the detritus of procrastination. Steven nudged me
about it periodically. He'd gone from being less keen on adoption than I to being, if not more so, at least more willing to discuss it. "I don't know if we'd actually do it," he would say, "but if
we *ever* want to consider adoption, I think we should start talking about it."

When Koko called again, a few days later, her voice was more
insistent. "A baby is going to be born that needs parents," she
said. "I'd like to know if you're interested." Again, I erased the
message. I told myself that it was too soon—two months—
after my last miscarriage, that I hadn't given the acupuncture a
chance. And surely that was part of it. As demoralizing as that
pregnancy had been, it had also occurred surprisingly close to
the previous one. Maybe I was on a roll.

"You *can* get pregnant," Risa had told me at my last checkup.
"No one can tell you whether you'll ever have a successful pregnancy, but no one can tell you that you won't." That surprised me;
it was so much less dire than what I'd heard from the specialists.
Although she made no promises, she held out possibility. "The
question is really how much you can stand," she added. "It's about
how long you want to keep trying to get pregnant versus how
much you want to get on with your life, start being a parent."

And that was the rub. In the swirl of drugs, surgeries, and
miscarriages, I'd somehow lost sight of *parenthood* as the goal.
In fact, I'd harbored moments of panic with each pregnancy,
wondering whether, now that I'd proven I could conceive, I actually

wanted the obvious end point. (Then I'd immediately berate myself for my negative thoughts, which were doubtless causing my *qi* to stagnate, killing my baby.) My compulsion to succeed, to "win" at pregnancy may have rolled over my uncertainty about motherhood—replacing it with a fear that illness and infertility made me less of a woman—but the ambivalence was never resolved. Now, given the opportunity to parent rather than be pregnant, I clutched. Certainly, despite my reaction to little Kenji, I still had concerns about adoption. Sure, this was rather sudden. Yes, I still wanted to try for a biological baby, but that wasn't the whole story: faced with an actual, flesh-and-blood child that I could parent right now, I wasn't ready to make the commitment.

The third time Koko called, I answered. "Um, I've been out of town," I lied. "I just got your messages."

"I thought so," she replied. "There is a girl in Hiroshima who is having a baby and would like it to be adopted by an American couple."

"Really?" I said, feigning excitement. "That's great. But we haven't even started the paperwork . . ." I trailed off.

"Maybe you could do that now."

"Okay, sure. How about if I talk to Steven and call you back in a day or two?"

A week later I ignored the sound of her voice on my machine; it was the coward's way of sending my own message.

And here is the shame of my shame: I didn't tell Steven about Koko's calls. My excuse, my twisted rationalization, was that I didn't need to. By then we had come up with a new plan and I was certain, absolutely positive, that this one would work.

10

DEAR PEGGY, DEAR FISH

———•———

Two burly security guards blocked my view of the concourse. It was April 2002, the first time I'd picked someone up from the San Francisco airport since the World Trade Center bombings; I had forgotten there was no longer open access to the gates. The guards eyed me as I craned to see over their heads, bobbing and weaving any way I could for a clear sightline. How would I find Jess? What if I didn't recognize her? I had seen pictures, of a slim, curvy young woman with expressive eyes, auburn hair, and a twenty-one-year-old's newly hatched skin. She'd warned me that she was short (which, as a person of height myself, I privately considered a character flaw), but even so, I aimed my gaze too high and would've missed her if she hadn't raised an arm to flag me, her cheeks pink-flushed, her smile glowing. I grinned back, but couldn't match her wattage. I was too busy looking her over, thinking to myself, *Could I really bear this woman's child?*

* * *

"I can't believe my luck! I really hope you're Peggy Orenstein the author!"

That was the first line of an e-mail I'd received five years earlier from a sixteen-year-old who identified herself only as "Fish." Girls often wrote to me in those days after reading *Schoolgirls*. Usually we traded a letter or two and that was it. But Fish kept writing and so I did, too. Eventually I learned her real name was Jess Catapano. She was the only child of an elementary school aide and a construction foreman in West Palm Beach, Florida, where she attended a specialized public arts high school. "I feel so lucky," she wrote. "I wouldn't be happy at all in a regular school." Jess loved writing and did it well; she dreamed of being a journalist someday, maybe focusing on feminist issues as I had.

She peppered me with questions about my career path and the courses I took in college. We traded recommendations for books (me: *Autobiography of a Face*; her: *The Bell Jar*) and CDs (me: Kelly Willis, *What I Deserve*; her: Death Cab for Cutie, *Something About Airplanes*). Sometimes she asked for more pressing advice: her friends were smoking weed—should she try it? She loved her boyfriend—was it time to have sex? I treaded carefully, not wanting to lose my credibility but afraid of over-influencing her. I felt more at ease (though also more account-able) when a year or so into our correspondence her mother dropped me a line. "Thank you for writing to Jess," she said. "It means a lot to her—and to me. It's good to know she has an-other trustworthy adult to talk to."

At first I only responded to Jess's letters rather than initiating my own, but after a while, especially if we had three or four exchanges a day, I lost track of who was propelling our correspondence forward. Jess was funny and talented; I enjoyed knowing what was going on inside of her head. More than that, as the miscarriages mounted and the IVFs failed, our exchanges made me feel that I had a hand in raising a child. I was thirty-four when we "met"; she was a high school junior. For the first couple of years, I was guarded about the details of my own life; I wasn't dishonest, but I didn't want to burden her with cancer and infertility—problems she was too young to understand. Once she was in college, though, I became less protective. In my work I'd said that the best role models don't try to present themselves as perfect; young women need honesty, not Teflon. I was determined to practice what I preached.

Jess was aware that I was trying to get pregnant—I had briefly mentioned my first miscarriage—but it wasn't until my second failed IVF attempt that I came clean about the months of infertility treatments. "I had no idea you were going through all that," she wrote. "I know it sounds strange, but if I were out in California, I would donate eggs to you!"

I smiled at her idealism, at the stalwart exclamation point at the end of her sentence. She still believed life should be fair, that there was justice. What a difference a nineteen-year age gap made. "Thank you," I wrote back. "Your offer brought tears to my eyes, but I don't think we would consider anything like that."

Jess wasn't the only person to say she would spot me a few gametes. My friend Catherine, an English professor in Des

Moines, also wanted to help. I love Catherine like a sister. Like me, she's tall and slim, with blonde hair and blue eyes. We read the same books, share the same politics. And I already knew her eggs did good work: she had two bright, handsome boys, one of whom was my godson, Max. I might have been tempted, but Catherine was already thirty-six; although her second son was born just a year before, the recommended cutoff age for donors was thirty.

"Wow," she said when I told her, "that makes me feel old."

"Tell me about it," I answered.

Steven had been hearing about Jess for years; I read him her letters, tried out my responses on him, especially on the morally sensitive subjects. "I think we should at least discuss it with her," he said, when I mentioned her latest e-mail. "I'm not saying we'd ever do it, but it seems like at this point we should move forward on all fronts."

"She's too young," I said, ducking the issue. "You have to be at least twenty-one, and she just turned twenty."

A few weeks later I left for Japan and realized I was pregnant. Then I had come home and got pregnant again. Each time, egg donation seemed blessedly irrelevant, so I gladly let the subject drop. A few months after the third miscarriage, though, when Jess gently reiterated her offer, Steven was more adamant. "We can keep trying on our own," he said. "But, Peg, we're getting old. If the point is to be parents, we don't have the luxury of doing one thing at a time."

I could have taken this opportunity to cop to my confusion, my distortion, over whether that indeed was the point; I could have confessed to secretly rejecting Koko Kondo. Doing that might have reconnected us as a couple, at least once Steven got over the betrayal. Instead I covered with yet more empty promises: "I'll talk to Jess about it," I assured him. Steven and I had busy lives: I was on contract with the *New York Times Magazine*; he was traveling back and forth to Santa Cruz, finishing his film. It was easy to let things slide, to let this latest evasion merge into the tension flowing between us, to create yet another eddy of resentment and resistance.

My fortieth birthday once again fell on Thanksgiving, though thankful was the last thing I felt. I looked in the mirror that morning, traced the lines on my face. No doubt about it: I was old and so were my eggs. I'd wasted the second half of my thirties lurching from crisis to crisis, the victim of my body's whims. Did I really want to lose my forties, too? I needed to let go of my obsession with getting pregnant, but if I did, what would keep me from freefall? I'd invested so much emotion, so much money, so much time . . . for what? There had to be a payoff.

Tossing away the condoms is one thing. Using someone else's eggs is quite another. But once you've awakened the desire to have a child; once you've stoked it in order to convince yourself to submit to drugs and surgery that cost tens of thousands of dollars, once you've further added the fuel of frustration and despair, considering an egg donor will eventually, inexorably seem reasonable. Not ideal, perhaps, but . . . possible. And it's hard to know, even now: did I really want to have a baby that way, or was I being swept along by a process— one in which, admittedly, I participated—of perpetually raised stakes and overly inflated expectations that I didn't know how to stop?

Either way, I began toying with a new narrative, one that felt revolutionary rather than compensatory. With a donor egg I could still feel a baby grow inside me, experience its kicks and flutters. I could control—that sweetest of words—the prenatal environment, guard against the evils of drug and drink. I could give birth to my own baby, breastfeed it. Who knew? Maybe for the child, that would make up for the genetic disconnect, maybe it would be less psychologically complicated than coming to terms with adoption.

Jess's twenty-first birthday was less than a week after my fortieth. When she brought up egg donation again, I mailed her a packet of information I'd collected, along with a letter about my experience with IVF: the discomfort and potential side effects of the shots, the risks of general anesthesia. I also told her I'd want her parents' approval. "I respect that you're an adult," I said, "but that's the best way I can think of to be sure you wouldn't have regrets later, that you wouldn't feel exploited." Meanwhile, I booked her a ticket to come to California for a weekend. "There are no strings attached," I told her. "It's a visit, not a commitment."

At the airport, we threw our arms around each other—the closest of friends who'd never met. We chattered nonstop on our way to the car, as we browsed the shelves of Sephora in downtown San Francisco, as we walked through the Chinatown gate and up into North Beach. Over foccacia sandwiches and tumblers of raw red wine at Mario's Cigar Store, Jess filled me in on her parents' response to her offer.

"They were totally unsurprised," she said, smiling at my amazement. "Can you believe it? My dad said, 'I figured you'd want to do that if you could.' I said, 'How did you know? I wasn't even sure myself.' And he said, 'I know what kind of person you are.' They asked a lot of questions about the process and the safety, but they were completely supportive."

My throat tightened. "If I ever have a baby, I'm calling your mom and dad for parenting tips," I said. "They're incredible."

Back on the street we scaled the phallus of Coit Tower, admired the fairy gardens that grow along the spine of Telegraph Hill. When I was single, these spots were the romantic staples of first dates. As with potential beaux, I couldn't keep from stepping back from the moment with Jess, observing our time together, wondering where it might take us. I found myself dissecting everything she said, everything she did. Her Italian American features looked kind of Jewish, I decided, though they couldn't have resembled mine less. Although that was superficial, it bothered me. On the other hand, I laughed at her jokes, admired her ambition, stood in awe of her generosity. I doubt I would've had the empathy or selflessness at her age to do what she was doing. I seized on every positive trait, genetic or not. Jess was well-mannered, appreciated her parents. She was a hard worker, too, selling furniture twenty-five hours a week to supplement her college scholarship. And, of course, she dreamed of being a writer, just like me, was already building her résumé through clips for the school paper and unpaid internships. All of that made me feel safer, as if the outcome would be more knowable.

"I do have one question," Jess said, as we were driving over to Berkeley. "Would you tell the child?"

171

"Absolutely," I responded. "Steven and I discussed that we'd want him or her to know you. If you want that, too."

She looked relieved. "That would be my first instinct, but it's totally up to you and Steven. If you want me to be involved, that would be great, and if not, I completely understand. You're not putting any pressure on me to donate, so I won't influence your decisions about what happens after the fact."

"What I'd really hope is that your relationship with the child would be like mine has been to you," I said.

Jess grinned. "That would make me so happy. Especially if it's a girl."

I began to imagine a child with Jess's kindness and Steven's artistic streak, with her silver-belled laugh and his warm eyes. Steven was considering it, too. "I think her features would mix well with Asian," he mused that night after Jess went to sleep. We'd each struck on the word "lovely"—not one we generally used—to describe her. Jess *was* lovely, and perhaps because of that, by the end of the weekend the three of us had fallen into something like love, just as one expects to before creating a family.

The morning that she left, I told Jess we'd like to try on our own a little longer. "I want to give it a year from my last miscarriage," I said. That would be in September, five months away. "If I'm not pregnant by then," I took her hand, "Jess, could I have your baby?"

She laughed. I added, "But I want you to know that you'd be free to change your mind at any point—even the day of the egg retrieval—and I'd understand. It wouldn't change our relationship."

"I want to do this," Jess insisted. "I really do. I have such respect and love for you and Steven. I know you'd be great parents."

"You realize you could go through all this for nothing," I continued. "The odds are in our favor, but it's not a given."

"Well," she said, "I guess we'll never know unless we try."

Dr. Dan e-mailed to say that he didn't need to see me unless we actually started a cycle. Meanwhile, the clinic's donor coordinator, Katherine, could answer any questions. She explained that donor cycles were like IVF, except split between two people, one providing the eggs, the other the womb. If we decided to move forward, Jess and I would go on the Pill for a month to sync our reproductive systems, then add a second drug to shut them down so the doctor could artificially manipulate them. A few days after that, Jess would start injections of nun pee and hamster eggs, while I would take a weekly shot of estrogen in my hip to thicken my uterine lining. She could be monitored by a doctor in Florida until a few days before the egg retrieval and would fly home the day after. Steven would do his thing, and when the embryos were ready, they'd be transferred to me. Then I would add a nightly shot of progesterone to my regime to trick my body into thinking it was preggers. If it all worked— and there was a 60 percent chance it would—I'd stay on the shots until the end of the first trimester. At that point, miraculously, my body would kick in and take over on its own for the duration. Easy-peasy.

Naturally, adding that third person to the mix upped our costs—if we were considering an "unknown donor," who would be compensated for her troubles, they would run well over twenty thousand dollars; with Jess, whom we insisted on giving a token amount despite her protests, they would be closer to sixteen. The clinic also required a legal contract between Jess and us as well as psychological screenings by their social worker to make sure we'd worked out all the ethical and emotional kinks. We agreed to get those things out of the way over the next few months; it couldn't hurt to be prepared.

"Jess is very mature, far beyond her years," the social worker said after their session, which she conducted by phone. "I was concerned when I heard how you knew each other—we don't consider a mentoring relationship appropriate for a known donor—but I can see that it's much more than that, more like the bond between an aunt and a niece. I'm satisfied that there isn't any coercion here."

I didn't fully share her confidence. This woman had talked to Jess for an hour. She was hired by the clinic, paid by the doctors—what was her motivation to turn away business? Regardless of what she said, of what Jess herself said, I remained uneasy. I believed I *did* hold a position of power in my relationship to Jess, one I didn't want to abuse. Was it truly possible for her to make this choice freely? I would never be sure.

There were a host of issues I couldn't resolve in advance. How could I know, for instance, what I'd feel when someone commented on how little—or even how much—the baby looked like me? Or whether I'd be jealous if the child felt some visceral connection to Jess? What if he or she turned to me someday and said, "You're not my *real* mother?" What if I agreed, felt like a fraud? There wasn't a lot of precedent here, no one among my friends to whom I could turn for guidance. I could let the uncertainty stop me, I decided, or I could stick with Jess's own words: We would never know unless we tried.

Three more months went by. I was still seeing Dr. Chang, but she'd stopped seeding my visits with photographs. She began to insinuate I wasn't sincere about reducing my stress, then to directly accuse me of not relaxing enough. Ever the passive-aggressive, I retaliated by canceling appointments at the last minute. One day, after going through the litany of questions about my bowels and bladder, she set down her pen.

"So," she said, "what do you want to do?"

I considered. I'd been through six months of Clomid, two rounds of IVF, three miscarriages, and a year of acupuncture. We'd spent over forty thousand dollars trying to have what we now called a "biogenetic" child. Each month I was convinced I was pregnant; each month I was crushed when I wasn't. Each month I had to confront my ambivalence, consider the question yet again: did I really want to be a mother? I wanted—needed—to get out of the spin cycle.

"We've been talking about trying donor eggs," I said, cautiously.

She nodded. "I think that's a good idea."

I promised to return to treatment when we started the cycle, but I knew I wouldn't.

"You should bring in the donor, too," was the last thing she said to me.

This time, sitting in the clinic's waiting room, I felt compassion rather than competitiveness. How many of these women had told even their closest friends they were here? How many were on their second or third go-round of IVF? How many were flattened by defeat and shame, yet still unable to stop?

Since our last visit, two years before, Dr. Dan and his colleagues seemed to have picked up a significant overseas trade. Several Japanese couples checked in with translators while we waited, and were promptly whisked away, probably to someplace with nicer chairs. Later I'd find out that IVF was highly restricted in Japan, and although it wasn't expressly illegal, a government committee of gynecologists and obstetricians forbade doctors to perform donor egg procedures. That drove couples to the West Coast, where a brisk trade in Asian American eggs had developed. The couples returned home pregnant, never mentioning how their babies were conceived. The Japanese were a lucrative clientele, paying upward of fifty-five thousand dollars for their treatments (though that included translators, transportation, and hotel)—no surprise that a number of local clinics courted them. Asian American donors, too, commanded a premium—as much as ten, even twenty thousand dollars a cycle.

We were here for a meeting with Katherine, to work out scheduling and sign contracts; this would be the last step before a final decision to forge ahead. So we were startled when someone else, a woman named Janet, came out to greet us.

"Katherine is on leave," she explained, cheerfully. "I'm her replacement."

"She didn't mention that when I made the appointment."

Janet smiled. "I took her place last week." As she motioned for us to follow her, Steven and I glanced at each other. I shrugged, *What else can we do?*

Janet's office was two stories above the street, furnished with a featureless desk and chairs. "Would you like me to close the blinds?" she asked as we sat down. We glanced at the office building across the street. Steven's eyes narrowed. "Why would we want you to do that?"

"Well, some people . . ." She trailed off, seeming uncomfortable.

"Some people what?" I touched a warning hand to his knee. This woman could be the key to our having a baby, we couldn't afford to alienate her. "We're not ashamed of this," he continued. "We're not pretending that it's something other than it is."

Had I been wrong to feel less furtive? Apparently, we'd entered the dark back alley of science. More than thirteen thousand women used donor eggs that year, but most would never tell—not their families, not their friends, not even the child. Secrecy had never crossed our minds; we'd agreed with minimal discussion that a person has the right to know his or her origins. Not that I thought openness would be easy. My parents, for instance, assured me they would love their grandchild no matter whose genes she carried—both of ours, neither of ours, or something in between. I knew they meant it in the abstract but wasn't sure they could pull off the particulars. My dad loved to crow, "It's in the genes!" when one of his grandkids excelled in school, sports, or music. I worried about how hearing those comments would affect our child. Or maybe I worried about how they would affect me. Yet if we didn't tell, we'd have to let a daughter believe she was at risk of breast cancer because I'd had it. And what about the pediatrician? My obstetrician? Any divulgence would be a risk. I couldn't imagine building a healthy relationship with my child on a foundation of deception.

As Janet ran through potential dates, it became clear that she wasn't familiar with our case, not even the basics. She initially assumed that Jess was for hire, not a dear friend, and was unaware that she lived across the country. I wasn't pleased, but I let it go. She kept talking as we reviewed a sheaf of paperwork: documents confirming our informed consent, specifying our wishes for disposing of any extra embryos, and agreeing to binding arbitration should legal disputes arise. We signed them all, partly because that's what people do and partly because we felt we had no choice. We knew it was no signatures, no baby.

I woke up in a middle-of-the-night panic thinking, *Would the baby be Jewish?* Judaism, as I've said, is traditionally passed down matrilineally, so even though Steven is a gentile, our naturally conceived child would have been 100 percent Yid. Could the ancient Talmudic scholars have anticipated the possibility of cleaving biology from DNA?

I called one of the rabbis at my parents' Conservative synagogue in Minneapolis. "The mother who carries the child determines the religion," he explained. The Committee on Jewish Law and Standards, the central authority of the Conservative movement, had actually issued a policy paper on third-party reproduction. They'd based their decision on the bonding and the health risks of pregnancy and childbirth, as well as the precedent that the baby of a gentile woman who converts mid-pregnancy is Jewish. That suited my needs but seemed insensitive in the larger picture. It would mean, for example, that a baby born to a Jewish survivor of uterine cancer who'd used a gentile surrogate to gestate an embryo created from her own eggs and her husband's sperm would have to be converted. Secular law uses "intentionality" as a measure—the person or people who initiated the creation of a baby are the parents, period. As relieved as I was to put the question aside, that approach seemed more humane.

The next night I jolted awake again remembering a school assignment one of our nieces had recently completed: a family tree detailing her ethnic background. How would our potential child approach such a task? A friend who was a public school teacher told me that most Bay Area schools consider such assignments obsolete. "There are so many variables here between adoption, step-parenthood, two mommies and a sperm donor, two daddies and an egg donor. . . ." Instead, children make a tree with themselves as the trunk, adding roots and branches of their choosing: stepfathers, a birth mother, an egg donor, an uncle, their pet hamster—whomever they consider family.

The morning I was to start the Pill, I wept. My feelings were so tangled: gratitude toward Jess, grief that I'd never see my smile on a child, the niggling sense that if we just tried once more on our own we would succeed. The fear that it wouldn't work. The fear that it would. It was this sort of indecision that had gotten me here in the first place.

"Peg," Steven said. "You're the only one who can figure this out. You're the only one who knows how doing this will affect you."

"I know," I said, miserably.

He watched the distress play across my face. "Okay," he finally said. "I'll tell you how I think of it. We have this opportunity because of you—because of the book you wrote that brought Jess to us; because you helped her and encouraged her as she grew up; because of her connection to you. So this baby *would* be part you, it would be possible because of you. I'd think of it like a sundae: one scoop of green tea ice cream, one scoop of spumoni, and you'd be like the chocolate sauce that brought it all together."

Maybe that was only a pretty rationalization, something he said to break through my paralysis, to help me process emotions that I couldn't work through myself. Still, I liked the image—it was something even a child could understand. This may not be the act of love I had hoped would create our baby, but it would be an act of love, nonetheless.

I popped the pill in my mouth, felt its sweet coating melt on my tongue.

"Then again," Steven added thoughtfully as I swallowed. "Maybe you would be the nuts on top."

By the time we picked Jess up from the airport again, I had fully embraced the fantasy of creating a brave new family. I imagined sweeping our baby off to Florida to visit his "other" grandparents, Jess spending summers in California with us, holidays that looked like futuristic versions of *Yours, Mine and Ours*. Steven and I would be older parents. Our child, most likely, would have no siblings—what good fortune to have this extra layer of love in his life. Rather than an object of pity, I recast myself as a maverick, a pioneer, roles with which I was infinitely more comfortable.

We had bought an extra ticket so Jess's boyfriend could join her for the first weekend of her visit; we expected she'd stay just a few days longer. Brian was an aspiring music producer, heavily into vinyl; Steven had closets full of LPs. (He'd sold off about a thousand to make room for me in his apartment when we'd moved in together, which I considered a more significant declaration of his love than our marriage vows.) The two of them disappeared into our den as soon as we arrived home.

I watched as Jess methodically prepared her nightly injections. Something immediately looked amiss. "I think you're using too much water to dilute the medicine," I said.

"No, Janet said it was one vial of water for each vial of powder."

"I'm almost sure that it's one vial for *all* the powder. Didn't anyone go over this with you in Orlando?"

"They said if I'd talked it through with Janet on the phone and read all the instructions they didn't have to." She looked worried. "I'm afraid to do it any other way without checking."

"Okay," I said, reluctantly. "But will you be sure to ask the doctor tomorrow?" She agreed, continued to fill the syringe brimful, and poked it into her thigh. It took nearly a minute to inject all that fluid. Although it had been two years since I'd done it, I was sure my shots hadn't been that big.

Dan was on vacation again.

"This is ridiculous," Steven fumed. "It's like he's a front man who ropes you in with his smooth bedside manner before passing you on to someone else."

"I don't know about that," I said, "but at least he could've told us."

It was Sunday and Dr. Franklin, who had done our last IVF, was out as well. Instead Jess saw a doctor we didn't know, a guy with a British accent who didn't bother to give her his name. She came back to the waiting room in tears. "He told me my eggs weren't developing fast enough," she sobbed. "And when I asked about overdiluting the medication, he yelled at me. He acted like I wasn't trying, like it was my fault."

Brian wrapped his arms around her, holding her tight. "I did exactly what they told me to do," she sniffled into his shoulder. "I'm a human being, not a chicken!"

"I'd say you're a human being, not a servant," I said, acidly. I didn't know how "unknown" donors were handled, but I expected Jess—my generous, trusting Jess—to be treated with respect. Not just respect, but with deference and appreciation for the great gift she was giving us. Later I complained to one of the nurses, who rolled her eyes.

"Oh, that one," she said, dismissively. "He's only here on weekends when the other doctors can't make it. She won't have to see him again." That hardly seemed like an excuse.

Jess was still shaky when we left the office. "I know what will make you feel better," I said. "Let's go to church!"

The two of them looked at me oddly: Jess knew I was Jewish, and Brian, a lapsed Jehovah's Witness, was leery of religion. But Steven had been doing a pro bono project at San Francisco's Glide Memorial Church, which billed itself as the most diverse, inclusive congregation in the world. The flock at its Sunday "celebrations" was a tonal rainbow of white and brown; a mix of homeless addicts and monied professionals; gays, straights, and transgenders; Jews, Muslims, Buddhists, and Christians.

Although nominally Methodist, Glide's message was universal: God was love, God was acceptance, God was the impulse to help those in need. And the gospel-style choir, with its live band headed by a one-time member of Sly and the Family Stone, rocked the house. When a slip of a white woman with a blonde ponytail and pipes like Aretha's knocked out "Love Train," we spontaneously leapt to our feet—levitated, really. As the four of us clapped and swayed to the music, merged with it, I thought, *A baby conceived in so much good will indeed be truly blessed.*

Sometimes you have to pay for hope, but that morning it came for free.

The "few days" Jess was supposed to be with us dragged into nine. Although it improved, Jess's egg production remained slow and her estrogen levels sluggish, making us all tense. Upping her dosages and diluting the meds properly helped, but not as much as we would've thought. And the twice-daily shots had become an ordeal; whether it was a side effect of the hormones or the stress of the process, they made Jess nervous and weepy. I'd thought of her as a levelheaded, competent young woman who knew precisely what she was getting into, but maybe that was simply what I wanted to believe. She was only two years out of her teens—how mature had I been at twenty-one?

Even as I hugged and comforted Jess, I fought the urge to turn away. I didn't want to see her vulnerability, didn't want to admit what this cost her. Watching her brace herself for the shots made me long for an "unknown" donor—that way I wouldn't have to see what I was putting her through. I grumbled to Steven that I had done everything Jess was doing and more without a fuss; it wasn't such a big deal. Of course, I was thirty-eight at the time, not twenty-one, and I was doing it on my own behalf, not someone else's. My impatience was unfair, I knew it, and I also knew it was a deflection from something else: despite my love and gratitude, I resented Jess, just a little, for being able to do what I could not. I would catch myself staring at her peachy, young skin or biting back a cynical response when she effused about her future. I envied her optimism, the confidence of her youth. It had been wishful thinking to believe that she and I could go through this without complication.

The morning of the egg retrieval Steven joked that he was feeling vaguely adulterous.

A flicker of jealousy tickled my gut. "Does that mean you're attracted to her?"

"No," he said, disgusted. "I'm just saying it's weird. Can't I tell you anything?"

"I still don't get it," I said, stubbornly. I was so alienated from my body, I had long ago discarded the notion that sex was in any way linked to reproduction; this was hardly the way I wanted it put back in.

"There were twenty eggs," I whooped when Jess woke up from the surgery. "*Twenty!* This might really happen!"

She smiled, groggily. "That's great!" she said. "I'm so happy."

On the way home, though, Jess was unusually quiet. "I don't feel very well," she said from the backseat, her voice quavering. By the time we pulled into the driveway, she was crying. "I feel really sick," she repeated, over and over. I led her into her room, tucked her in bed, shut the door. Then I burst into tears myself, paced the living room floor, frantic. How could I have put someone I love through this?

"Why weren't you prepared for how hard it might be for her?" Steven chided. "We're talking about a young person here. You should've thought this through."

"But I always felt fine after the surgery. It never bothered me."

"Well, the clinic should've prepared her better, then. The social worker should've done more than one lousy hour on the phone with her. How could that be enough?"

Jess's parents phoned awhile later; she was asleep. "She's doing okay," I told them. "I think it was harder than she expected, but she should feel better by tonight."

"That's good to hear," her mother said. "I know how much she wanted to help you. And we want to express our support, too, because we know how much you want a family and we feel so fortunate to have our one, wonderful kid. Good luck to you, Peggy."

Jess left early the next morning. I was ready for her to go, eager to cast off the guilt and responsibility, to be a couple rather than a technological ménage à trois. Yet, as soon as the plane took off, I missed her terribly. If the social worker had overstated our relationship before, she was right about it now: Jess was like a niece, like a daughter, one of the closest people to me in the world. No matter what happened, we were bound for life. Whether I became pregnant or not, she was part of me.

"I meant to ask," Steven said, as we drove home from the airport. "Were they supposed to do ICSI again?"

That was the procedure Dan had advised last time, in which individual sperm were injected into the eggs. "I'm not sure," I said. "Why?"

"Because when I brought the sperm to the lab the technician asked about it. I said, 'Aren't you supposed to know?' I told him he'd have to ask the doctor."

"No one ever mentioned it," I said, my mind still on Jess. "I guess if they're supposed to do it, they will."

I grabbed the phone on the first ring. "Things didn't go as we'd hoped," Dr. Franklin reported. It had been twenty-four hours since the egg retrieval, and only four of the eggs had fertilized.

"*Four?*" I repeated, dully. "How can that be? There were *twenty.*" Instead of homing in on Jess's eggs, Steven's sperm had just lain there in the Petri dish doing the backstroke. Even as the bottom dropped out of my stomach, I recalled his comment about infidelity. *Maybe,* I thought with a surge of affection, *his boys just couldn't go through with it.*

Steven's sperm may have been an issue all along, the doctor added, but the problem was masked by my age and egg production. I remembered the giddiness I'd felt years before when Steven's first semen analysis seemed off, the urge I'd had to wear a sandwich board reading, "It's his sperm, not my career." That thought was cold comfort now.

"So what are our chances?" I asked, steeling myself.

Dr. Franklin was quiet for a moment. "Maybe thirty percent?" That was less than half of what it had been yesterday— and I got the feeling he was being optimistic.

The situation had worsened by the time we came in for the

transfer. Dr. Franklin inserted all four embryos into my uterus, but none had progressed well. He offered little hope of success.

"I don't understand," I said. "Why didn't you do ICSI again?"

He shook his head. "I don't know. That was Dr. Balfour's decision. It was probably done before because of low egg production and quality, not because of Steven's sperm."

"But he's had borderline sperm in the past—Dr. Balfour knew that. He never even talked to us about it."

"He probably should have," Dr. Franklin said, then seemed suddenly uneasy. "In retrospect one always wishes one had sat down and discussed it."

Talk about inhospitable wombs; I was so upset that I couldn't sleep. I couldn't eat. And the fact that I couldn't eat or sleep (which I was convinced was lowering my chances of success even further) made it even harder for me to eat or sleep. And round and round it went. Sometimes I was sure I felt pregnant: my breasts were tender, my uterus ached, but I knew that could be an illusion perpetuated by the nightly progesterone shots Steven was giving me. My hips bloomed with wine-colored bruises, and I could no longer sit for extended periods. That didn't matter—even if I'd been numb from the waist down, I wouldn't have been able to keep still.

The results were no surprise, yet I spent the day on a crying jag. It was over. Our last, best chance, the one that seemed our destiny, had failed. Worse yet, I felt betrayed by the clinic. In retrospect the whole cycle seemed mishandled—from the coordinator's inattention, to our doctor's unexplained absence, to the shoddy treatment of Jess, to the decision against ICSI.

I should've noticed. I should've stopped it. But I trusted Dan; now, in addition to barren, I felt victimized.

I called Jess, feeling almost as bad for her as I did for myself. "We're not pregnant," I said.

"Oh, I'm so sorry."

"No, I'm the one who's sorry. I'm sorry about all you went through, all I put you through."

"Don't think twice about that," she said, staunchly. "I'll never regret it. It was important to do, whatever the outcome. Otherwise we would always wonder."

"I guess so," I said, though I was left wondering anyway.

My grief was thick and dull, punctuated by the occasional stab of panic. Trying again was not an option; I could never ask Jess to do that. What next? Adoption? Childlessness? I didn't want to think about it. I moved my computer into Steven's office to avoid being alone during the day. After work we took long walks through the Berkeley hills, not saying much. Breathing in the hot, eucalyptus-scented air of yet another Indian summer was the only time I felt lighter.

Steven was stoic, as usual. I misread his response as indifference. "That's not it," he insisted one afternoon as we hiked along a ridge. "But thinking about the lost opportunity, the disappointment, that sense of hope that turns to sadness—it fills me with such despair that I'm afraid if I let it in, I'll be incapacitated. It's like those moments in college when I'd be sitting alone in my apartment not knowing what I'd make of my life, eating ramen noodles and feeling nearly suicidal. But I'm older now. I know those feelings pass, that they're normal.

And we have each other"—he took my hand, his voice growing soft—"and we love each other, and I know that good things lie ahead for us. So right now I just want to keep moving forward."

I smiled. "That's weird," I said. "I've been thinking about my twenties, too, that feeling that I'd never find someone to love who loved me back, of being so empty and alone.

"I'm going to be sad for a while, hon," I continued. "Maybe for a long time, but I really do know that as long as we're together I'll eventually be happy again."

In that moment of connection, it finally felt right to admit that Koko Kondo had called. "I'm sorry," I said. "I know it was wrong that I didn't tell you about it."

Steven stopped walking. "That's not just *wrong*," he replied, "it's one of the most dishonest things you've ever done in our relationship. It's unfathomable. I mean, what if you reversed the situation, if you wanted a child and we couldn't have one and one day over dinner I told you that I'd refused Koko months ago without even telling you about it?"

"I don't know what to say. I guess I'm a bad person."

I watched Steven's face as anger gave way to resignation. "It's not that you're *bad*, Peg," he said. "It's that you don't have the courage to be close, to trust each other."

I nodded morosely. "I'm sorry," I repeated. "I really am."

Steven sighed, shaking his head. "Why don't you call Koko and tell her we're still interested?"

"Okay," I said. "But do you think you could do it instead? I can't face her."

"Why? You're the one who knows her."

"I'm too ashamed. Besides, you understand the cultural subtleties better than I do.

"Also," I added, "Maybe we should wait a little while. I feel so raw; I think I need a little more of a shell before I can move on."

"We don't have that kind of time," Steven said, the edge creeping back into his voice. "We have to move forward now if we ever want to do it."

I nodded again. "But I don't know if I can ever get past the regret that it took me so long to realize that I wanted to have a family with you," I said, my voice trembling.

"You have to, Peg," Steven said. "The only way to survive this is to be grateful for the two of us, for what we have together."

Steven did call Koko the next day, but although she was understanding, she wasn't encouraging. "She said she has no idea when she'll get another baby," he reported. "It could be years. Also, there are four other couples ahead of us." He looked at me, accusingly. "It seems we missed the boat. We can't count on this."

He didn't have to say any more; the facts were punishment enough.

I made a list of our complaints and read them off to Dan at our follow-up visit. "It seemed like there was no one at the helm during this cycle," I concluded, my voice level. "Like no one was making decisions. And the worst of it is we've lost the chance to have a baby with Jess. This was a unique situation, a special relationship that we'll never be able to replicate. It's a *huge* loss for us."

Dan nodded sympathetically. "We can't say for sure the cycle would've worked had things been different. But I agree that we bear partial responsibility for the failure." We said nothing, waited him out. "Let me talk to my partners about what we could do to make it right," he finally said. "I'll get back to you in a week or so."

"Thank you." My appreciation was genuine. His responsiveness hadn't staunched my sorrow, but it had alleviated the rage—that was something.

While we waited we sought a second opinion from Marcelle Cedars, a friend of Risa's, who a year earlier had been named director of the University of California at San Francisco's infertility clinic. I liked Marcelle immediately. She had the same direct, sisterly style as Risa, the same feminist commitment to women's health. "Look at this," she said, pointing at the records we'd brought her. "The semen analysis they ordered just before your second IVF came back with only four percent morphology."

"What does that mean?" Steven asked.

"It's the shape of the sperm. Fourteen percent is normal. This would indicate a low likelihood of fertilization."

"I don't remember anyone ever telling us that," I said. "So you're saying they should've done ICSI this round, too?"

Marcelle nodded. "I would've. But I see a few other issues as well. Your uterus hadn't been evaluated in four years. I would have done that. And personally, I would have had the donor take her shots in the muscle rather than under the skin—I find that the response to stimulation is better that way. I also would've had you use a skin patch rather than shots for the estrogen. A lot of people do the injections, but I think the patch is more effective."

"How can two doctors have such different ideas?" I asked. "Does that mean his was wrong?"

"Well, this semen analysis would concern me," she said. "But a lot of the variation is about the art versus the science of medicine. It has to do with the lack of full data in this area—there are very few randomized trials in our field to let us know what works best so people develop their own preferences. The Europeans say it's like the Wild West over here."

Maybe if I'd had Marcelle as my doctor, I thought, *I'd have a baby right now.* She seemed to read my mind. "I could do a quick ultrasound to check your follicles and see if it might be worth trying another round of IVF," she offered as we got up to leave. "Or have you closed that door?"

"We have," I said, but I suddenly felt it creak open a crack. What if the problem had been Dan's protocol, or merely the insensitivity of the clinic's doctors? In a flash I was cobbling together the money, dismissing the emotional devastation that grew worse with each miscarriage, each failed medical intervention. It would be crazy to try again. But I felt that flutter: what if it worked?

"I suppose," I said, casually, "it wouldn't hurt to look."

I undressed and lay on the exam table, unsure what I was hoping for. Marcelle inserted the ultrasound probe, then shook her head. "You made the right decision," she said. "There are only two follicles developing here, and the best we could do is double that. Four follicles isn't worth putting you through it again."

Was I relieved? Sure. Was I sorry? Absolutely. I was also shocked that no one had suggested this simple, inexpensive test before. If we'd known way back before starting the first IVF that my production would be so paltry, would we have gone ahead? Would we have approached the process differently? I tried to push those thoughts aside—it was done. "But I am going to ovulate again, aren't I?" I asked. It had been over a month since the donor cycle, and although I'd bled when I went off the shots, I had yet to get a natural period. That wasn't unusual, but I was eager to get back to normal.

"Not for a while," she responded. "These follicles are very small."

Two weeks went by with no word from Dan. I left him a voice mail reminding him of his promise, then e-mailed a few days later. In the brief reply I finally received, his tone seemed to have changed; instead of the concern he'd shown in his office, he seemed distant and self-protective. "We can offer you a repeat donor oocyte cycle at the rate of $3,500," he wrote. That would not, he continued, include "outside costs" such as a new donor, the medications, anesthesia, or what he referred to ambiguously as "etc." Adding that all up, our end cost would still run at least thirteen thousand dollars beyond the sixteen thousand dollars we'd already spent. That's if we were interested in using an unknown donor—and if we were interested in working further with Dan. Neither, by now, was the case.

I felt like the high roller whose new friends disappeared when his stake was gone. The caring brochures, the chummy smiles, the warm affect of the clinic "team" seemed abruptly stripped away, revealing nothing more than a cold-blooded business. We had wanted so desperately to believe that we had ignored the sales pitch in the compassion, the coercion in the photographs of babies and sunflowers. But I finally got it— these guys may have been doctors, but they were also salesmen. I may have been a patient, but I was also a consumer. I was undergoing a procedure, but I was also making a deal—and they were making a buck.

Dan's offer was an insult; what's more, we felt he ignored our pain. We shot back a letter detailing what we'd learned from Marcelle, with a veiled threat of legal action if we didn't get a full refund. I didn't realize that fertility docs are pretty much bullet-proof. Back in 1978, when Louise Brown, the first "test tube baby" was born, IVF was as controversial as cloning is now. In her excellent book, *Pandora's Baby*, Robin Marantz Henig writes that opponents—particularly antiabortion activists who considered the destruction of unused embryos akin to genocide—successfully lobbied to ban federal research funding on the procedure. Ironically, that, along with insurance companies' refusal to pay for it, drove IVF into the private sector, where it has enjoyed minimal consumer regulation or ethical oversight.

In perhaps the most notorious subsequent scandal, the founders of one of the country's top fertility clinics, at the University of California at Irvine, transferred fertilized eggs from as many as three hundred patients into other women's wombs without their knowledge. Two of the doctors subsequently fled the country; a third was charged with mail fraud—there were no laws against using a woman's eggs without her consent. And as recently as 2005, the medical license of one of San Francisco's preeminent fertility specialists was revoked after he transferred the wrong embryos into a patient, then covered up the mistake for over two years. The gestational mother is now embroiled in a custody battle with the couple whose embryo created her son. The embryologist involved, once again, saddled up and fled the country. Yee-haw.

The lawyer I consulted about our situation said it's difficult to sue a doctor when there are no standard practices in the field. "One of the bedrocks of California law is that a doctor's not liable for doing something another doctor might do, even if they're in the minority," he said. "I wouldn't waste your time and money. You'd never win."

That was the year I returned to the synagogue on Yom Kippur, fasting and wearing white in search of a new beginning. I joined my new friend, Ayelet, and her husband, Michael, in the pews (which, given the holiday's prohibition against bathing and deodorizing, lived up to the name). Like most of the women I gravitated toward then, Ayelet understood loss; she and Michael had terminated a fetus after amniocentesis revealed a chromosomal abnormality. Even now, several years later and pregnant with their fourth child, she hadn't fully come to peace with that decision.

Before each segment of a Torah portion is chanted, someone has the honor of reciting a blessing, called an *aliyah*. At this temple, rather than singling out four or five individuals, *aliyot* were meted out by concept. So, for instance, the rabbi asked anyone who had worked for peace over the last year to come forward. People crowded the aisles to participate. Then he called up anyone who hoped in the next year to "create life, or bring something new into the world." Ayelet leaned toward me, looking like a *Star Trek* princess in her white caftan, round belly, and copper-colored hair. "Let's go up," she said. "You stand next to Michael. I call him 'The Sperminator.' He can get anyone pregnant."

The three of us stepped into the aisle, which was already jammed. Ayelet stood on one side of Michael, I stood on the other. He lifted up his woolen tallis so that it covered all three of us like a tent. I leaned in, holding Ayelet's hand behind his back, my free hand touching the shoulder of the person in front of me, who was in turn touching the shoulder of the person in front of her, and so on until we were all connected to the person who actually touched the Torah scroll. Then I closed my eyes and chanted words I hadn't sung for years but that always lived inside of me. I didn't know if I would ever have faith, but perhaps I could find solace.

"This is Koko Kondo . . ." At the sound of that voice on our machine, Steven lunged for the phone. It was the last Thursday of October and we were packing for a long weekend in San Francisco. We thought a few days of playing tourist in the city would relax us, give us a chance to reconnect.

"She says there's a high school girl in Hiroshima who's pregnant with a baby boy and would like him adopted by an American couple," Steven told me, after hanging up. "The other couples on her list want girls. I told her it didn't matter to us. He'll be born next month. She wants to know if we're interested."

"Are we?" I stammered

"I told her we'd have to discuss it."

"We still haven't done any of the paperwork," I said, but my excitement was rising. Maybe my instinct upon seeing baby Kenji was right, and this was indeed our destiny—a child from Japan, from the country of Steven's ancestors; a baby who came to us through a personal connection, through our joint good work in Hiroshima. That made sense to my writer's brain, to its insistence on a narrative of fate.

"I still have the home study questionnaire," I said. " I could bring it with us. We could get started on it over the weekend."

But we didn't. The paperwork sat on the desk in the hotel room just as it had sat on my desk at home. It wasn't that we were unwilling at that point; we just needed time off. So we saw *The Ring* at the megaplex. We ate *teppanyaki* in the Tenderloin and house-made pasta in Union Square. And we shopped; we went to FAO Schwarz and bought early Christmas and Chanukah gifts for our nieces and nephews. I hadn't bought clothes in over three years, convinced it was a waste since I was surely about to get pregnant. Now I indulged in retail therapy of the first order, splurging on a three-quarter-length leather jacket at Coach and a boiled wool blazer at Armani. I didn't care what they cost—looking fabulous was my consolation prize for not having a baby.

On Saturday morning we strolled through the Farmer's Market at the Ferry Building, snacking on organic strawberries and holding hands like the lovers we'd once been. We laughed. We had fun. We didn't talk about babies. It had been a long, long time. That night Steven embraced me. I resisted at first, still estranged from my body; then consented, for his sake; and finally, gazing out at the city lights from our hotel room bed, I gave in to the feeling.

Steven was supposed to call Koko back that Monday, but didn't get around to it for another two days. It was November 5, 2002, barely a week since her last phone call. When he hung up, he looked pale.

"What is it?" I asked.

"She said the baby's been born," he responded. "He's been born and they need a name from us so he won't go on the birth mother's *koseki*." A *koseki* is a real-life version of the mythical "permanent record" so often invoked to keep American high school students in line: a set of official documents marking a family's births, marriages, deaths, and other milestones. Although the information is supposed to be private, it's readily accessible to potential employers and go-betweens arranging a marriage. An illegitimate birth could destroy a young woman's future, but if we named the baby, giving him Steven's last name instead of the biological mother's, the child would never be recorded on her *koseki*, as if the pregnancy hadn't happened. But we would have to act immediately.

Steven and I stood in the hallway, looking at each other in silence. "Well, Peg," he finally said. "What do you think we should do?"

11

KAI-*CHAN* ACROSS
THE WATER

We named him Kai, of course. Kai for the ocean that separated us. Kai for the ocean that would bring us together. The few details Koko provided about his background were reassuring. His birth mother was a junior in high school. Her parents were divorced. She lived with her father, who hadn't noticed the expanding bump she'd camouflaged with extra-baggy clothes. When she was seven months along, she confided in an aunt who took her to Dr. Miyoko Kohno, a female obstetrician in Hiroshima, who, coincidentally, was an outspoken advocate on behalf of troubled teenage girls. (*More kismet,* thought I!) The girl had never seen her baby—whether that was by choice or unfortunate custom Koko didn't say. Kai had spent a few days on a maternity ward and was now being fostered by Koko's mom and sister. He'd weighed a respectable seven and a half pounds at birth and was over twenty inches long. On the advice of a friend, we asked for his Apgar scores, whatever they were—some mark of responsiveness at birth, I gathered. At any rate, they were normal. We asked if the birth mother drank, if she did drugs, if there was mental illness in the family.

"Japanese only put healthy babies up for adoption abroad," Koko said, sounding slightly annoyed. "Although sometimes we send the other ones to someplace like New York." I couldn't tell if she was joking.

There are so many children out there who need homes. That refrain had echoed in my mind throughout our infertility treatments, growing deafening during the donor egg cycle. Why were we going to such extremes to create a child when *there are so many children out there who need homes? Why*, as people would occasionally ask me, *don't you just adopt?* I had my responses (including, "Why don't you?"), but only now did I discover the most obvious one: adoption isn't so easy. The *children out there who need homes* are older or have special needs; I wasn't prepared to take on those challenges. Later I would learn that, domestically, as many as forty couples can vie for a healthy, white newborn (though a white child wouldn't have been a priority for us). International adoption is uncertain, expensive—upward of twenty thousand dollars—and, where Americans benefit by others' poverty and oppression, involves its own ethical complexities.

Then there's the adoption process itself. We would have to open our lives to an agency's scrutiny (paying thousands of dollars for the privilege), which involved three visits by a social worker to evaluate the fitness of our home. Our official "dossier"—an appropriate name for something so relentlessly nosy—had to include the questionnaire that I'd avoided for so long; tax returns and bank statements, a full reckoning of our finances and spending; multiple character references from old friends; copies of our birth certificates and marriage license; employment verification; and proof of housing and health insurance. We would also need medical exams; we were told by one agency that my cancer history could disqualify us, as could my visits to a shrink after my third miscarriage—thank heavens I hadn't taken any psychotropic drugs. We'd need both state and FBI fingerprints to prove we weren't child molesters. Various documents needed to be notarized, then brought elsewhere so the notarization could be authenticated. All of this, pursued diligently, typically took four months; it could take another five for the backlogged Immigration and Naturalization Services (INS, today renamed Citizenship Immigration Services) to approve the application.

Generally, prospective parents would wait up to another year to be matched with a specific child. But we already had a baby waiting. "There's got to be a way to speed up the paperwork," I told Steven, grimly. At his urging, we bought tickets for a flight to Japan, leaving in three weeks. I planned to have powered through the red tape by then.

Strangely, there was no listing in the phone book for the San Francisco office of INS. The Web site said that we'd be denied entry to the building without an appointment, yet offered no way to schedule one with the adoption division. I called the Washington, D.C., office for help. A friendly (and apparently newly hired) agent promptly gave me the number for the local director of orphan petitions.

She didn't even say hello. "How did you get this number?" she hissed.

I apologized politely and explained our situation.

"I can't help you," she said, adding that scheduling our FBI fingerprinting alone would take up to a month.

"What if I brought over the paperwork personally?" I tried.

"You can't."

"But we have a baby waiting," I said.

"You *can't.*"

After several more rounds of this, she grudgingly told me to write "Do Not Open in Mail Room" on the envelope containing our filing fee and initial forms. "That might speed things up some," she said. I didn't ask why the mail room was opening her letters in the first place.

"Could I have your name? Then I could address it directly to you."

There was silence at the other end of the phone. "Hello?" I said. "Are you still there?"

More silence. And then, "It's Bernice, but if you put that on the envelope it will only slow it down.

"And remember, *never use this number again.* And don't give it out to *anyone.*" With that, the phone went dead.

Right around that time I read about a toy company that was marketing a line of "girl positive" action figures as alternatives to Barbie. One of them, a snowboarder, was supposed to have been adopted. Her accompanying "biography" said, "Someday she wants to find her real parents, but in the meantime she rescues pets." I shot off a letter to the company's founder: "I don't dispute the loss that some children who were adopted feel," I wrote, "but the people who walk the floor with a child when she's sick, who weather her tantrums, kiss her boo-boos, celebrate her birthdays, attend her school plays—the people who are actually *there* are her 'real parents,' don't you think? To imply otherwise under the guise of 'empowerment' is offensive."

Honestly, though? If I hadn't been trying to adopt myself, I probably wouldn't have noticed.

My indignation may have been legitimate, but it was also a reflection of my insecurities: I wasn't sure whether I would feel like Kai's "real" mother. Koko FedExed us a photo taken moments after his birth. There he was, naked on a baby scale, his arms and chicken legs flailing, his eyes screwed shut, his mouth a rictus. His head, with its patchy black hair, was squeezed into a point from its journey down the birth canal. I looked at that squalling, outraged creature and felt . . . nothing. Was I supposed to love him on sight? Was I supposed to know that he was my son? Who was this child, anyway, and what were we signing up for?

"All of that is horrible to contemplate," agreed my friend Deborah, who had adopted her two children. "But it will all go away as soon as you have the baby—*your baby*—in your arms. Being a parent is so much more powerful than any of those fears. You'll just forget about them."

I wanted to believe she was right, but I kept thinking about the disproportionate number of adoptive boys with learning disabilities, behavioral problems, criminal records. "Adoption *is* scary," said another friend, a psychologist who had herself been adopted. "I won't tell you it's not. In the end, though, you have to accept that you can't have control over everything. Whether you give birth or whether you adopt, Peggy, parenthood is all about surrender."

There was a problem. Japanese babies bound for San Francisco weren't being allowed in the country. Bernice had frozen all further adoptions, rejecting the documentation the Japanese used to declare a child an orphan. "I know of three families so far who've had difficulties and there may be more," said Susan Kawamoto, an acquaintance who'd just adopted her second baby from Japan. "It's only in San Francisco. Nobody's having trouble in Sacramento or San Jose. And there's nothing wrong with the paperwork. We adopted our daughter three years ago with no problem, and nothing has changed except the person running the agency." As far as the Japanese were concerned, Susan and her husband had been their son's legal guardians since birth, but she'd spent five months trying to convince Bernice of the same. In the meantime, Susan's son had been parked in a maternity ward in Tokyo, at a cost to her and her husband of a hundred dollars a day.

"It was awful," she told me. "I wasn't allowed to contact Bernice directly. I couldn't even get her phone number. There are protocols for everything, and no one wanted to break the rules." She tried pleading with the Japanese Consulate, but they refused to intervene. Even her local adoption agency abandoned her. "Bernice is the gatekeeper for all international adoption," Susan said. "It was like they didn't want to jeopardize their relationship with her over one child. There are so few adoptions from Japan, maybe it didn't seem worth it."

Working through various intermediaries, Susan finally convinced Bernice to meet her in the lobby of the INS building. "She claimed she was being extra cautious because the Cambodia program was recently shut down over charges of baby selling," Susan said. "It was ridiculous. As if all Asian countries are the same. The situation in Japan is nothing like Cambodia. But I didn't argue, because if she wanted to, she could throw up obstacles forever."

Although Susan eventually managed to get her son home, the other parents she knew hadn't, so far, been as lucky. "There's no way of knowing whether you'll *ever* be able to get your baby out, Peggy," she said. "I'm so sorry."

At that moment my hesitations vanished. I had a cause again. The grief, anxiety, and fury I'd felt during the previous five years turned molten: no way in hell was some government flunky going to keep me from my child. I called the head of Asian adoption in Washington, but even when, out of desperation, I dropped that I write for the *New York Times*, he wouldn't interfere with what he termed a "local matter." We looked into changing our address to Steven's mother's in L.A. or my parents' in Minneapolis, but that wasn't practical; we'd have to start the home study again with another agency and there would be questions about why we'd moved so suddenly, why our tax returns and employment were in the Bay Area. If we explained, those officials might decide to reject the adoption as well.

Next, I tried our political connections: former vice president Walter Mondale, who'd been an ambassador to Japan, was an old law school buddy of my dad's; Steven was friendly with Norman Mineta, who was, at the time, secretary of transportation, the only Democrat in the cabinet of the first Bush administration. Surely, one of them could pull some strings. Our agency cautioned against it. "Going over Bernice's head could antagonize her," the social worker warned. "She might make things even harder."

Bernice seemed untouchable. There was no way to know whether the adoption would go smoothly, be delayed for months, or could happen at all. What's more, Koko's mother, kind and generous as she was, was in her eighties; she couldn't care for a newborn indefinitely.

"Maybe you should go to Japan until we can bring him home," Steven suggested.

"How would that work?" I asked. "Where would I live? And for how long? And what if we couldn't get him back at all—what would I do then?" I tried to imagine being alone with a newborn in a foreign country. "Oh God!" I moaned. "I can't believe we're going to lose another baby."

"Peg," Steven said, sharply. "You've got to stop defining yourself through tragedy."

My eyes widened. "But this *is* tragic."

"You have to learn to appreciate the opportunity no matter what happens."

"How am I supposed to do that?"

"Well," he said. "I always thought if I had a child, I'd go out and buy two baseball gloves, a big one and a little one. Because it takes a long time to break in a glove. And I'd oil them and work on them so they'd be perfect when he or she was ready. And I feel like if I did that for Kai, even if the adoption didn't work out, I'd be grateful for the time I had oiling the gloves and imagining him as my son."

I wished I could share Steven's attitude, that a few days' fantasy about playing ball with my child felt worth having my heart shredded yet again. I admired him for it in the same abstract way that I admired his composure when faced with the mountain lion, but it wasn't me.

I lay awake that night, spinning on the hamster wheel of my thoughts. "Kai-*chan*," I whispered into the darkness. "Are you my son? Am I your mom? We've worked so hard these past few weeks to find out. We've tried every way we could to be sure we'll be able to bring you home, if this is your home.

"And even if it's not, we'll always be the ones who named you."

My forty-first birthday fell five days before our trip. I'd been feeling bloated and bitchy all week—industrial-strength PMS, I figured. It had been two months since the donor cycle and I was still waiting for my period.

On a whim, I peed on a leftover pregnancy test. I held the result behind my back as I walked into the bedroom. "Remember that romantic weekend in San Francisco?" I asked Steven.

A glance at my expression and he knew. "You've been pregnant before," was all he said. "This doesn't change a thing."

Two babies. One baby. No babies. When I told my mother, she offered to move in with us for six months. A friend joked, "You'll have Irish twins!" And I—I who was never sure I wanted

even one child—was terrified. *Two babies. One baby. No babies.*
The refrain beat a tattoo in my head. I didn't know what would
happen; I didn't know what I wanted to happen. Over the next
few days I forgot two interviews, left my wallet at the supermarket, ran a red light. I showed up at a friend's house for a
party a day early all dressed up with a pan of overcooked
brownies. I was lucky nothing worse occurred.

"What should we do?" I asked Steven. "I already feel so invested in Kai, but I don't think I can handle more than one
baby. Besides, our house is too small. And the cost of private
schools . . ."

"Well, do you want to abort?" he said.

"Of course not! I wouldn't. I couldn't."

"Do you want to give up Kai?"

"And risk ending up with nothing? I don't think that's an option." Surprisingly, I didn't have a strong preference for a biological child over Kai; or perhaps more correctly, I was afraid to
have one. The baby within, as I'd come to think of it, was too
precarious, impossible to believe in after three losses. Kai was a
real, living child; he'd already insinuated himself into my dreams.
I found myself wishing the pregnancy, and the problem, would
disappear. On the other hand, if I had to go through one more
miscarriage, one more D&C, I thought I would surely go mad.
"Is it wrong that I feel more scared than anything else?" I asked
Steven. And to myself, I added, *Does it make me a bad mother before I've even started?*

At the FBI office, would-be Americans sat in rows of hard
plastic chairs, filling out forms for green cards and watching

Regis Philbin bray from a TV bolted to the wall above them. A security guard looked at our appointment slip, then pointed, unspeaking, to a blue line painted onto the dirty linoleum. We followed it upstairs to a second waiting room, and when our names were called, into a third. When it was my turn a woman grabbed my hand and pressed it onto a computer screen. My fingers were cold and damp; it took several tries to get it right.

"How long will this take to process?" I asked.

She shrugged. "Maybe a few weeks. Maybe a couple of months."

How could that be, I wondered bitterly, *when a fifteen-year-old could get our criminal record in ten minutes on the Web?*

Driving home, Steven suddenly burst into laughter.

"What's so funny?" I asked, startled.

"Do you realize that we both just drifted off in the middle of a conversation?"

He was right: I'd stopped speaking mid-sentence, become lost in thought. It had taken him ten minutes to notice.

"This is really the test of how stress affects pregnancy," I said, dryly. "I've never been so overwrought in my life. If the baby within can survive this, it can survive anything."

Although nothing was certain, we decided to go to Japan and hope for the best. Steven had lots of friends in Tokyo; maybe one of them had the connections to get us around Bernice. We went to Baby Gap and bought Kai a warm hat, a blankie, a teddy bear. I held up a white romper trimmed with yellow duckies. "This may be for our son," I told Steven, and he smiled. A friend insisted I borrow her baby sling in case we wanted to take him for a walk. "Can't we just carry him in our arms?" I asked.

She looked at me pityingly. "You have a lot to learn," she said.

We converted five thousand dollars into yen to cover Kai's stay in the hospital as well as Koko's and the Tanimotos' expenses. "Pack the camera in the carry-on," I told Steven, "so we can take pictures of ourselves going to the airport and getting on the plane." Maybe we couldn't give Kai a birth story, but we could tell him the tale of how Mommy and Daddy came to Japan to meet him.

It was the day before Thanksgiving and the airport teemed with babies. They were perched in their strollers, snuggling in BabyBjörns, ferried onto planes that, like storks, would whisk them to the arms of loving grandparents. I averted my eyes, unwilling to let myself believe that next year, one way or another, I would be among them. I panicked when the plane's engines started. Some studies have shown that stewardesses have abnormally high rates of miscarriage. What if the radiation on the flight killed the baby I was carrying? I tried not to think about it. I tried not to think about anything, but as I held Steven's hand, I recalled that other trip, so long ago, when we first decided to try to conceive, when I still had the arrogance of the ignorant. I never imagined I'd end up here, never imagined I'd put myself through so much for something I wasn't even sure I wanted. But rolling along the landing strip, I realized: I did want to be a mother. I wanted it badly—wanted the love, the delight, the vulnerability, the boredom, the surprises, all of it. I wanted to find out who parenthood would make me. I had just become afraid to admit it, even to myself. As we took off, I felt the plane's vibrations in my teeth. I gripped Steven tighter, but said nothing.

We dozed most of the way across the Pacific, waking in what was, with the time change, early evening on Thanksgiving Day. As we approached Osaka, the plane banked to the left. The man in front of me turned around, his headphones still on, and pointed excitedly out the window. "*Fuji-san!*" he said. I looked down at Mt. Fuji's perfect, snow-tipped cone glistening with the deep plums and corals of the setting sun. Dawn on the mountain is called "Buddha's Halo." I've never seen it, but it couldn't be a more glorious or tender sight than this one.

"The view makes me want to climb it," Steven said, and I nodded. The sacred spirits, or *kami*, of the mountain are reputed to heal pilgrims, both body and soul; that sounded good to me. The trouble is, five thousand people a day make the trek during climbing season, littering the trails with trash and sewage. I suspected we were better off admiring the mountain from this silent, abstract distance. As the peak faded from sight, I remembered reading that *Fuji-san* is actually three mountains. The lava from Shin-Fuji, the one we could see, had buried the other two. It was the mountain's most enduring lesson: sometimes you have to dig deep to discover the truth.

He was so tiny, so very tiny—only three weeks old. Chisa Tanimoto, Koko's mother, gently settled Kai into my arms and I gazed into his eyes. I'd never wanted to love someone so much in my life. In the picture Steven snapped at that moment, my expression is a tug-of-war between excitement and apprehension.

The previous night, we'd met Koko in Osaka; she'd told us we were expected to take Kai with us, keep him in our hotel room for our three days in Hiroshima. "But we don't know anything about taking care of a baby," Steven protested.

She was firm. "You'll learn," she said. "Kai needs to be with his parents."

Koko's mother and sister didn't speak much English. They demonstrated how to diaper the baby, pantomimed how to prepare his bottles. They indicated we should feed him every four hours, no more, no less. Then Mrs. Tanimoto wrapped Kai in a blanket, handed us a pack of supplies, and called a cab. I cradled him carefully, feeling a bit like a girl playing dress-up in her mother's clothing, clomping around in oversized high heels and smudged lipstick.

"What should we do now?" Steven asked, back at the hotel.

"I don't know. Maybe get some lunch?" It took our full combined effort to wedge the baby into the sling. He seemed content there, nestling against the warmth of my body, though I checked him every few seconds to make sure he hadn't suffocated. I wrapped my jacket around the two of us and we walked through the Peace Park, the branches of the cherry trees now winter bare. As with the last time I was pregnant in Japan, I found the smell of the local cuisine sickening—a particular torment since eating there was one of my greatest pleasures. Instead, we chose an Italian restaurant that was largely patronized by middle-aged salarymen and their young, female companions. Kai slept on the banquette next to me while we ate. The waitresses cooed over him, and later another couple with small children noticed us and smiled. It was kind of fun, this business of being parents.

That is, until the sun went down. At six o'clock Kai began yowling like a wet cat, his mouth stretched wide, his face an angry tomato. We changed his diaper, gave him a bottle (though it was not yet "time"), but nothing helped. Worse yet, jet lag was starting to hit me along with the heavy-limbed queasiness of pregnancy.

"I'm sorry, Honey," I said, handing the wailful bundle to Steven, "but it's time for a crash course in fatherhood." I put in earplugs and passed out.

For the next eight hours, Steven paced the small patch of hotel room floor. Sometimes he took a break and sat in front of the TV, dandling Kai on his knee, but the baby never tolerated that for long. A bottle would soothe him briefly, but soon he'd be at it again.

I took over around two in the morning. "What is it, little guy?" I asked. Maybe he was colicky, or gassy. Maybe he was simply fed up with being passed from person to person—he'd had three homes in as many weeks—and longed for the smell and taste of his mother. *One baby. Two babies. No babies.* I tried to imagine pacing the floor with a newborn while helping a nine-month-old adjust to a new home, a new country, a new language, new parents. The notion left me numb. *One baby. Two babies.* Sometime around daybreak, Kai dropped off to sleep and so did I. Steven snapped our picture again, curled up together on top of the blankets.

Things were much the same for the next two days. Kai would

sleep cherubically in his sling while we roamed Hiroshima, then, come sunset, Baby Hyde would emerge. On the third night, Steven woke me at twelve. "I can't do this anymore," he said, dumping the infant in my arms.

I sat up, propping Kai against my knees so we could examine each other. "Poor sweetie," I crooned. "You must be so confused."

Miraculously, he grew quiet at the sound of my voice. I snuggled him against my chest; he burrowed his face into my neck. I eased my body lower, until we were both lying down. As long as I held him close, he slept. "Poor sweetie," I whispered again. Sometime over the next few hours as I listened to his freight train breathing, I felt something in my heart release. I didn't know what was right anymore, didn't know what we ought to do, but I knew that I could love this baby; I knew he could be my son.

The next morning, we returned Kai to the Tanimotos. As we drove away, Koko's nephew held the baby aloft like a flag. I looked back, waving vigorously through the cab window until we were out of sight, all the time wondering whether I would ever see him again.

We spent our last afternoon in Hiroshima trying to find out whether we could file our forms directly with the U.S. Embassy in Tokyo, bypassing San Francisco INS. Steven phoned his various connections with no luck. I, meanwhile, tried a fellow named Suzuki whom Koko had suggested. He turned out to be a lethal combination: Japanese and a functionary.

"If you filed here," he told me, "we would have to send the forms to the regional office in Korea. It could take a long time."

"How long?" I asked.

"I don't know."

"Weeks? Months?"

"I don't know. Maybe it is better to file where you live."

"I live in San Francisco," I said.

"There have been problems in San Francisco," he observed. "Families that cannot bring a child into the country."

"I know," I said.

"We are trying to address this matter."

"How?" I asked.

"We are preparing a response."

"What kind of response?"

"I don't know."

"Do you think you can resolve the matter?"

"I don't know."

"So then maybe it's better if we file in Tokyo?"

"Yes, but we may still have to contact San Francisco INS if there is a problem."

"What kind of problem might there be?"

"I don't know."

"What could we do to avoid the problem? Are there papers we could have?"

"I don't know."

"So what would you advise we do?"

"It is best to file where you live."

"But we live in San Francisco."

"There have been problems in San Francisco. Families that cannot bring a child into the country."

What is the sound of one hand slamming down the phone?

The Gigo Arcade in central Hiroshima is four stories of wholesome family fun. The first floor features interactive games involving virtual sports cars and motorcycles. On the second floor, teenage girls pose in photo booths, holding up their fingers in peace signs. Middle-aged men chain-smoke on the top floor, gambling for tokens at video poker, blackjack, and horse racing. I favored the third floor, with its four-foot-high Tetris screens. For a hundred yen a pop, I could maneuver the falling blocks neatly into place. *Two babies. One baby. No babies.* They were so much more manageable than the pinballs caroming around in my head.

"What if we struggle for nine months and the adoption is still denied?" I fretted to Steven as we wandered back to the hotel. "Or what if it comes through and I'm too pregnant to fly over here and get him?"

Steven was quiet for a moment. "I think we have to consider stepping aside, Peg," he finally said. "There are too many variables. We need to tell Koko to look for a family outside of San Francisco."

My eyes swam. "Could we at least ask her to wait six weeks until we find out if the pregnancy is viable?" In January I was scheduled for a chorionic villus sampling (CVS), an early form of prenatal testing that rules out chromosomal abnormalities, such as Down syndrome, that are more common among children of older mothers. If the results were normal and I hadn't yet miscarried, my chances of having a healthy baby were as good as anyone's. Besides, by then the dispute with Bernice might be resolved.

"Peggy," Steven said, softly. "It's not fair to leave Kai in limbo. You know it's not. We need to tell Koko to start looking now."

The words he'd spoken a few weeks before floated back to me. "I really am grateful to have had this opportunity," I said, sniffling. "It was nice to be his mom and dad, wasn't it?"

Steven nodded. "Yes, it was."

The hotel room seemed weirdly hushed without Kai. We undressed, not saying much, and lay in bed together feeling lost. *Two babies. One baby. No babies.*

The next morning, we went home.

A chart at the prenatal testing center showed a steep rise in fetal abnormalities as a woman ages. Only one in a thousand thirty-year-olds would have a baby with Down syndrome. At my age, eleven years older, three in a hundred would.

"But think of it this way," the genetic counselor told us. "There's a ninety-seven-percent chance the baby is fine."

Steven squinted at the chart again. "Ninety-seven percent?" he said. "Then why don't we just assume it's normal?" He was right, but by then I had no faith in luck, no truck with probabilities. What were the chances that I would have gotten cancer? That I'd have three miscarriages? What were the chances that I'd be sitting here pregnant in the first place?

In CVS a doctor, guided by ultrasound, inserts a long, hollow needle through your abdomen (or sometimes your cervix) and withdraws cells from the developing placenta. It's similar to amniocentesis, though less comprehensive—it doesn't, for instance, show the presence of neural tube defects such as spina bifida. The test also causes a slightly higher rate of miscarriage than amnio—about three percent, equal to the odds of actually discovering an abnormality. The procedure doesn't hurt. Or, more accurately, by the time I registered the pain, it had already passed, the needle was in. After that the discomfort was more psychological: I just prayed the doctor didn't sneeze.

We called Koko that night to tell her we'd get the results in a week. "That's okay," she said, cheerily. "I've already found new parents for Kai. They're in San Diego and their paperwork is all ready."

I caught my breath—I didn't expect this so soon. Since no one else on Koko's list had wanted a boy, I'd thought we might still have the chance to change our minds if the test went badly. *One baby? No babies?* Our safety net was gone; then again, a child shouldn't be a safety net, should he? I mouthed a silent good-bye.

"But guess what?" she added. "They liked the name Kai. They've decided to keep it."

We were still in bed when the phone rang. I was sure it was the doctor's office with the CVS results.

"Aren't you going to answer it?" Steven asked. I shook my head; I was too frightened to move. "I can't," I whispered. "I just can't."

He shoved his feet into his slippers and trudged down the

hall. "Hello," he said, picking up the phone. "Yes, it is. Mmm-hmm. Mmm-hmmm. Mmm-hmmm. Okay. Thank you."

Time stopped. I had the sensation of looking down from a great height, though I didn't know at what. Motherhood? Childlessness? Where would the next plunge take me? Steven's face, when he returned, gave away nothing. *This is the second before I know how I'll spend the rest of my life*, I thought. I stared at him, wordlessly.

He grinned. "Everything's fine," he said. "And it's a girl."

EPILOGUE: MEDITATIONS ON LUCK

If she had been a boy, I would've called her Isaac, which in Hebrew means "he will laugh." The biblical Sarah concocted that name for her son in response to God's first practical joke. She was ninety years old when the child was born, making me, at forty-one, feel a mere sprout. Instead, we chose something equally whimsical: Daisy Tomoko (the latter Japanese for "friend"). She is the joy of our lives.

One morning about a week after her birth, as she and I strolled through our garden to fetch the day's mail, my eyes fell on a small, stone Jizo statue partially veiled by ferns. I'd bought it from a monastery in Oregon almost two years before to mark my third miscarriage. Seeing it always startled me a little, like the prick of a pin. I wasn't sure whether to bow my head before it or chuck it in the trash. That was pretty much how I felt about everything that had happened over the previous six years— torn between a need to remember and the desire to forget.

A manila envelope nudged open the top of the mailbox. Its return address was marked "Immigration and Naturalization Service." "IT HAS BEEN DETERMINED THAT YOU ARE ABLE TO FURNISH PROPER CARE TO AN ORPHAN," read a letter inside. Although we'd abandoned our attempt to adopt, we'd paid our fees, filed our forms, so the bureaucracy had kept churning. It had taken until now—exactly nine months since Kai's birth—to clear the first hurdle; we still would have had to get him past Bernice. I shuddered to think of what that time would've been like for us. I had thought about Kai often, particularly now that I held another infant in my arms. We had only spent a short time together, he and I, but I missed him. I still do. For months I couldn't bear to develop the photos we'd shot in Hiroshima. When I did, I shuffled through them once, my throat constricting, then hid them away in the back of a drawer. What else was there to do? I couldn't exactly frame them, but I'll never throw them away.

Walking back to the house, I recalled that Jizo is supposed to guide a *mizuko* toward another try at life, either with the same woman or with another. Maybe, then, I wasn't meant to be Kai's mother. Maybe he had tried three times to be born through my womb but failed, then tried once more through someone else's. Maybe when he found his true mother in San Diego, my body was finally free to make Daisy.

I floated that theory past Steven. He looked at me gravely. "Never repeat that to anyone," he said. "You sound like one of those whackos."

* * *

221

"Aren't you glad it all worked out?" I asked him another day. We were sitting on the couch taking turns holding Daisy, mesmerized by her cherry lips, her pearly toes.

His eyes narrowed. "Don't go getting revisionist on me," he said. "I don't want you to forget what actually happened and start thinking it was all worth it."

"I'm not," I protested. "I'd never do that." But I knew I was busted: I'd been busily rewriting our history in my head so that the end justified the means. As much as I love our daughter, I don't believe that's the case. I can't lie—the act of giving birth was surprisingly redemptive. Popping out a healthy baby at nearly forty-two (conceived with only one ovary!) not only restored my confidence in my unreliable body, it made me feel invincible. What's more, as it turns out I adore being a mom, though I'm a little uneasy saying so. I resent that to prove we're good mothers, professionally accomplished women are expected to claim that motherhood is our "most important job" or the "best thing I've ever done." Still, sometimes, sitting at a miniature table, covered in Play-Doh and reading *Where's Spot* for the thirty zillionth time, I don't recognize myself—and that's not a bad thing. Identity, I've learned, can be sliced many ways and there is gain with every loss. At least, under the right circumstances. Just as he expected, Steven is as involved and competent a parent as I am. It's because of that fluidity, and the freedom it brings, that I don't, as I feared, feel personally or professionally compromised by motherhood. Not that it's effortless—simultaneously keeping a marriage vital, being a parent, and pursuing a demanding career is, as I anticipated, a complicated hat trick—but we do it together. For me, that's made all the difference. And watching Steven chug through the house pretending to be Thomas the Tank Engine with our daughter bobbing around on his shoulders fills me with a delight I've never known.

Even so. Becoming a parent can't give me back the time—the entire second half of my thirties—obliterated by obsession. It doesn't compensate for the inattention to my career, for my self-inflicted torment, for trashing my marriage. Although my relationship with Steven has, thankfully, proven resilient, hairline cracks remain. We may never reclaim the ease of our early years together; all we can do is move forward—tenderly, kindly, with mutual forgiveness. And with the knowledge that our love for each other has never, ever flagged.

What if the deux ex machina of pregnancy hadn't descended upon us? That question haunts me. Would I have pushed to adopt Kai despite the obstacles? Could I have made peace with childlessness? Would I have ultimately destroyed the most precious, sustaining thing in my life: my marriage? I'd hate to think that the only way I could have righted myself was to have a baby. I'll never know whether that was the case.

Nor, short of "move to Sweden," would I know what I'd tell a young friend—say, Jess, who, as I once was, is now a twenty-five-year-old aspiring magazine writer in New York City. Do I wish we'd tried to conceive earlier? Sure, in a way, but then again, I'd hate to have missed all I did instead during those years: traveling the world, publishing books, enjoying the adventure of my marriage. And who's to say the outcome would have been different? If life gave do-overs, I wouldn't change my course, but I would choose to traverse it differently—with less craziness, more equanimity, more courage. I would tell myself, "This is your life, no matter what happens," rather than, "This is your life, only if you can make this *one thing* happen." Would that have made a difference? Could I have hung on to that thought once conception had become pathologized, once I was caught in the vortex of persuasive doctors and miracle cures? I don't know. That's the insidious thing about infertility treatments: the very fact of their existence, the potential, however slim, that the next round might get you pregnant creates an imperative that may not have otherwise existed. If you didn't try it, you'd always have to wonder whether it would've worked. That's how you lose sight of your real choices, because the ones you're offered make you feel as if you have none.

There were more than a million fertility-related medical appointments made within the last year, and it's unclear how many of them are necessary. One recent large-scale study found that 90 percent—*90 percent*—of women in their late thirties will get pregnant within two years of trying (assuming their partners are also under forty). Yet infertility in this country is defined as failure to conceive after just *one* year, and many couples, as we did, storm the clinic doors after just a few months. So what's a girl with a ticking biological clock to do? Until the workplace and family life better accommodate mothers, there's no right answer. Nor can you count on the specialists to provide one; their doctor-patient relationship is too easily influenced, if only subtly so, by profit motive and the vagaries of self-regulation. As ever-newer "cures," such as the recent hype over egg freezing, are dangled before us, it's up to the consumer to be alert to their pitfalls, to the allure of perpetual hope. I wish I had understood that.

Early on, a friend smiled at Daisy, lying milk-drunk in my arms. "Everything happens for a reason," she observed.

I bristled. That's not something I believe, not when women I love die leaving babies behind, not when children are starving, when adults are tortured. Nor do I like its corollary: "God only gives you what you can handle." If so, God is a sadist. I refuse to view life through such a simplistic, superstitious lens, whether it's held up by religion or by New Age. I did not get cancer because I held in anger. My infertility was not a result of my ambivalence about motherhood. Nor did I ultimately get pregnant because I was trying to adopt. It's a cruel myth that adoptive parents (presumably more relaxed once they've given up on a biological child) are subsequently more likely to conceive than other infertile couples: the rates for both are between 3 and 10 percent. In fact stress, that bogeyman of modern maladies, may be less relevant to both cancer and infertility than previously believed. A 2005 Swedish study examining stress before and during IVF treatment found that it had no negative impact whatsoever on success rates. The tightly wound conceived as readily as the calm. Meanwhile, a Danish study of more than six thousand women found those who were highly stressed were nearly 40 percent *less* likely than others to develop breast cancer.

Adversity is a random, arbitrary thing, though one can still glean meaning from it, use its crucible to become a better, more compassionate person. My story, I've found, is not so unusual. Many women experience at least one of its twists—miscarriage, infertility, breast cancer—and fear, at dark moments, that they caused their affliction. Most women ask themselves at one time or another what it means to mother—what the cost might be to their careers or marriages, how it reshapes the self. And all of us, male and female, encounter pain and loss; all of us reckon with dreams unfilled, with the limits our younger choices have placed on our later lives. All of us have to figure out how to move beyond that regret.

Nine years ago I considered myself a lucky person. But what I meant by that was that I was unmarred by fate, so mine was a callow good fortune. Even after cancer treatment, I resented the assumption that I ought to be more appreciative of life than my healthier friends. Since when was moral superiority a required outcome of illness? I was only thirty-five then, not ready to acknowledge life's fragility. I still believed I could fly through it on my Palm Pilot, scheduling stops for marriage and childbirth on my own terms. But now I wake up every day—*every day*—feeling transcendently blessed. Don't get me wrong. I still curse out drivers who leave their left turn signal on for three miles; I'm still irked by the grammatically inexplicable phrase "Can I help who's next?"; but my pettiness is dwarfed by a sense of reverent, radiant gratitude that's sweeter for having experienced its opposite, as love is sweeter for one's scars. Mine is the luck of realizing that happiness may only be the respite between bouts of pain and so is to be savored, not taken as an entitlement. I suppose I've finally understood the concept of *wabi-sabi*. And although in many ways I'd give a lot not to have learned it, I'm grateful for the lesson.

ACKNOWLEDGMENTS

I am indeed a lucky woman. I have always had friends, family, and colleagues who supported and guided me, held hope for me when I had none. I send you all my deepest love.

In particular I'd like to thank Suzanne Gluck, who with equal skill advised me on writing a book proposal and calming a fussy newborn; Bloomsbury's Gillian Blake (editor extraordinaire) and Karen Rinaldi (who shares my opinions about Manhattan in the 80s); all of the Orensteins and Okazakis; Barb Swaiman; Eva Eilenberg and Eric Stone; Ruth Halpern and Marc Halperin; Peg-bo Edersheim Kalb; Ayelet Waldman and Michael Chabon; Sylvia Brownrigg and Sedge Thomson; Susan Faludi; Kate Moses; Susanne Pari; Laurie Abraham; Elly Eisenberg; Dan Wilson and Diane Espaldon; Sandy and David Brown; Larry and Beth Brown (and all the kids); Rachel Silvers and Youseef Elias; Karen Stabiner; Terry Hong; Judy Fred Campbell; Jay Martel and Sarah Hemphill; Catherine Taylor; Lucy and Paula Arai; Risa Kagan; Katarina Lanner-Cusan; Marcelle Cedars; Rebecca Epstein; Madeline Licker Feingold; Ari and Kristin Baron; Brandon Wu; Kay Itoi; Sara Corbett and Mike Paterniti; Doug McGray and Carrie Donovan; Doug Foster (despite the move); Annie Lamott (despite the Barbie); David Fallek; Fumiyo Kawamura; Connie Matthiessen; Lisa, David, and Donna Cericola; Julia Eilenberg; Michael Pollan; Deirdre English; Susannah Grant;

Natalie Compagni Portis; Teresa Tauchi; Peggy Northrop; Neal Karlen; Aaron Brusso; Elliot Dorff; Deborah Gordon; Debra Condren; Lori Gottlieb; Lilly Krenn; Charlotte and Ken Gray; Anna and Marty Rabkin; Robert Bokelman; Susan Kawamoto; Kent and Mari Nagano; and Karen Nagano and Kenji. Thanks also to Ilena Silverman, Katherine Bouton, and Gerry Marzarati for their encouragement and patience, and to Ingrid Rubis for her gift with children.

The Japan Society's United States-Japan Media Fellows Program and the Asian Cultural Council awarded me generous travel and research grants. Special thanks to Ruri Kawashima for easing the transition to Tokyo, and to Veronica Chambers and Jonathan Alter for championing my Fellows nomination. I could never repay the charming and insightful Mihoko Iida for her patience with my endless dumb *gaijin* questions. And a most heartfelt *domo arigato goizaimasu* to all of those who helped me navigate Hiroshima, including the tireless Tomoko Watanabe (after whom Daisy Tomoko is named), Masako Unezaki, Yumi Nekomoto, Katsukuni Tanaka, Michiko Yamaoka, and the many other *hibakusha* who gave so generously of their time; the Tanimoto family, and especially Koko Tanimoto Kondo, who has brought love into the lives of so many.

My love, too, to Kai-*chan*, wherever you are, whoever you are. I think of you often and wish you joy.

And most important, my gratitude to and love for Steven Okazaki and Daisy Tomoko Orenstein Okazaki, who remind me every minute of every day that grace happens.

A NOTE ON THE AUTHOR

Peggy Orenstein is the author of *Schoolgirls: Young Women, Self-Esteem, and the Confidence Gap* and *Flux: Women on Sex, Work, Love, Kids, and Life in a Half-Changed World*. A contributing writer to the *New York Times Magazine*, her work has also appeared in the *Los Angeles Times*, *USA Today*, *Elle*, *Vogue*, *Discover*, *MORE*, *Parenting*, *Mother Jones*, *Salon*, and the *New Yorker*. She lives in the San Francisco Bay Area with her husband, Steven Okazaki, and their daughter, Daisy Tomoko.

READING GROUP GUIDE

Peggy Orenstein was never sure she wanted to have children—she loved her life the way it was. And through her work, as an acclaimed journalist and the author of *Schoolgirls: Young Women, Self-Esteem, and the Confidence Gap* and *Flux: Women on Sex, Work, Love, Kids, and Life in a Half-Changed World*, Orenstein had seen exactly how difficult parenting can be, how easy it is for women to lose themselves in their newfound status as mothers. So it's no surprise that it took five years of marriage—and countless discussions with her husband, who did want kids—before she finally made up her mind that yes, she was ready to be a mom. And then she got breast cancer.

Over the next six years Orenstein did almost everything humanly possible to have a baby, starting with "fertility sex" and escalating to high-tech Assisted Reproductive Technology (sometimes involving the purified urine of postmenopausal Italian nuns), along with several attempts at international adoption. The story of how she finally does become a mother is funny, honest, and deeply, achingly accurate. Any woman who has ever struggled with infertility or questioned her own maternal instincts will laugh—and cry—in recognition on every page.

For discussion

1. The subtitle of this book covers many of the milestones on Orenstein's journey to motherhood. In your opinion, which was most significant? Why?

2. On page 3 Orenstein says, "I'd had no idea how easy it would be to lose all sense of reason, to do things I swore I never would to become a mother, then go further beyond that." Have there been instances in your life when you have done this, whether or not they are fertility related?

3. Orenstein's husband, Steven, wants children because, as he says on page 8, "I think of life as kind of like an amusement park…If you're going to go, you should ride every ride at least once. And having kids is like the big, scary roller coaster. You can have a good time without riding it, but you would've missed a significant part of the experience." Is this an apt description of parenthood?

4. In explaining her ambivalence about motherhood, Orenstein says on page 11: "The issue wasn't whether I wanted to turn into my mother if I had a child or even whether I feared I would; it was that I believed I *should*." What did she mean by that? How did her experience researching her books color this expectation? How do you feel about motherhood in regard to your own mother?

5. Many of Orenstein's concerns seem to be about identity—as one woman says to her on page 97, "Once you become a mother, you're *only* a mother." In your experience—as a mother, a friend, a daughter—how has that proved true? And false?

6. What does feminism have to do with Orenstein's journey to motherhood? What about class issues? Politics?

7. The idea of destiny plays a large role in Orenstein's thinking. How did it affect her decisions? Have there been times in your own life when you believed destiny was a key factor?

8. Shrines of one sort or another also recur throughout the book. Why do you think there are so many different kinds of fertility-related totems? Do you think they helped Orenstein in her quest, or encouraged her obsession, or served another purpose entirely?

9. Reread Orenstein's definition of the *Eishet Chayil*, "the original woman who does too much," on page 49. How have the implications of the term changed over the years? Do you consider yourself a modern-day example? If not, do you know someone who is?

10. Discuss Steven's role in this story. Does your opinion of him change, and why? Why do you think their relationship was able to withstand so many years of stress?

11. In Japan, which has one of the highest abortion rates in the world, there are shrines where women can honor their aborted or miscarried fetuses. Compare the Japanese approach to fertility, abortion, and miscarriage with our own. Which did Orenstein feel more comfortable with, and why? What about Steven? And you?

12. What is your understanding of the term "wagamama" (page 97)? How does it apply to women in this country compared to how it applies in Japan?

13. Discuss the significance of Orenstein's trip to Hiroshima, beginning on page 116. How does it relate to the idea of destiny?

14. Compare Orenstein's attitude toward adoption to her husband's. Why does it seem like a relatively simple decision for one, but not the other? How do their attitudes change over time, and why?

15. On page 225 Orenstein is upset when a friend suggests that "Everything happens for a reason." Why was she bothered by this assertion? How do you feel about it?

16. At the very end of the book, on page 226, Orenstein says, "Mine is the luck of realizing that happiness may only be the respite between bouts of pain and so is to be savored, not taken as an entitlement. I suppose I've finally understood the concept of *wabi-sabi*." Reread her definition of the term on page 126—what do you think helped her to finally understand it? Is that a good thing? How might *wabi-sabi* apply in your own life?

Suggested Reading

Adopting After Infertility by Patricia Irwin Johnston; *Love and Infertility: Survival Strategies for Balancing Infertility, Marriage, and Life* by Kristen Magnacca; *Unsung Lullabies: Understanding and Coping with Infertility* by Janet Jaffe, David Diamond, and

Martha Diamond; *A Little Pregnant: Our Memoir of Fertility, Infertility, and a Marriage* by Linda Carbone and Ed Decker; *Sweet Grapes: How to Stop Being Infertile and Start Living Again* by Jean W. Carter and Michael Carter; *The Bitch in the House: 26 Women Tell the Truth About Sex, Solitude, Work, Motherhood, and Marriage*, edited by Cathi Hanauer; *Waiting for Birdy: A Year of Frantic Tedium, Neurotic Angst, and the Wild Magic of Growing a Family* by Catherine Newman; *The Mommy Myth: The Idealization of Motherhood and How It Has Undermined All Women* by Susan Douglas and Meredith Michaels

Peggy Orenstein is the author of *Schoolgirls: Young Women, Self-Esteem, and the Confidence Gap* and *Flux: Women on Sex, Work, Love, Kids, and Life in a Half-Changed World*. A contributing writer to the *New York Times Magazine*, her work has also appeared in the *Los Angeles Times*, *USA Today*, *Elle*, *Vogue*, *Parenting*, *Discover*, *More*, *Mother Jones*, *Salon*, and the *New Yorker*. She lives in the San Francisco Bay Area with her husband, Steven Okazaki, and their daughter, Daisy.